|5

Dublin Burning

The Easter Rising from Behind the Barricades

By the same author
With the Irish in Frongoch

Dublin Burning

The Easter Rising from Behind the Barricades

Commandant W. J. Brennan-Whitmore
Director Field Intelligence, 1916
Officer Commanding North Earl Street Area, 1916

Foreword by Patrick M. Geoghegan
Introduction and Notes by Pauric Travers

Gill & Macmillan

Gill & Macmillan
Hume Avenue, Park West, Dublin 12
with associated companies throughout the world
www.gillmacmillanbooks.ie

© The estate of the late W.J. Brennan-Whitmore 1996, 2013
978 07171 5930 7

Index compiled by Helen Litton
Typography design by Make Communication
Print origination by Carole Lynch
Printed and bound by ScandBook AB, Sweden

This book is typeset in Linotype Minion and Neue Helvetica.

The paper used in this book comes from the wood pulp
of managed forests. For every tree felled, at least one tree
is planted, thereby renewing natural resources.

5 4 3 2 1

Contents

Dedicated to the memory of Anna Josephine,
beloved wife and comrade

Foreword

William James Brennan-Whitmore has been described as the 'thinking man's revolutionary: long-haired and didactic, determined to have an important part in the campaign for independence'.[1] He was the only senior participant to leave a memoir of the 1916 Rising and, as a result, this unique document is an important and illuminating primary source. Indeed, its republishing in this 'decade of commemorations' provides a perfect opportunity to reflect on many of the debates surrounding this critical moment in modern Irish history, in particular, the role of the leaders and the objectives of the rebellion. Brennan-Whitmore completed his memoir in 1961, although it remained unpublished until 1996. The last surviving commandant of the 1916 Rising, he is described in the *Dictionary of Irish Biography* as 'an ultra-conservative idealist disappointed by the revolutionary legacy'. Written with the benefit of hindsight, and influenced by his own experiences post-independence, his memoir none the less contains many honest reflections and challenging insights. It is an important starting point for anyone interested in entering into—and trying to understand—the world of the men and women who fought in 1916. The traditional view of the leaders of the 1916 Rising is confronted here. There is no pious adulation of dead heroes, nor is there an attempt to score

---

[1] Patrick Long, 'William James Brennan-Whitmore', in James McGuire and James Quinn (eds), *Dictionary of Irish Biography* (9 volumes, Cambridge, 2009). (*http://dib.cambridge.org/viewReadPage.do?article Id=a9017*)

easy points off them, but there is an engagement with the reality behind the reputations. Patrick Pearse, a close friend, is praised as the 'head and font' of the rebellion, but Brennan-Whitmore also suggests that writers and historians had overstated his significance in the aftermath of the rebellion. Indeed he suggests that 'insofar as it was in the power of one man to bring an Irish insurrection into forthright activity, the credit for that achievement must go to Thomas J. Clarke'.

James Connolly emerges from the pages a strong and determined leader, fatally undermined by his mistaken belief that 'Capitalists will never destroy capitalist property'. He and Brennan-Whitmore, a Volunteer leader who occasionally attended meetings of the military council, clashed almost at once. Soon regarded 'as a bit of a nuisance', Brennan-Whitmore set himself the task of writing a textbook for the Volunteers based on his military ideas, and he went back to the tactics employed in Wexford during the 1798 Rebellion, as well as by the Boers during their conflict with Britain.

What becomes clear is that the leaders of the 1916 Rising were divided over the aims of the rebellion, and what could be achieved. One group believed that success was impossible, but that a 'blood sacrifice' would rouse the people from a state of apathy caused by years of parliamentarianism and relative peace. A second group looked to achieve a military victory, and was determined to start fighting only if there was a reasonable chance of success. Brennan-Whitmore was firmly in the second camp, but was disappointed to discover that the 'blood sacrifice' group was securely in control. Therefore the decision was taken to seize key locations in Dublin, and stand fast. Instead of 'an active and enterprising defence' the rebels became immobile, and Connolly is blamed for tying the post commanders too rigidly to the defence of their positions. Brennan-Whitmore does not doubt that Connolly had military genius, but suggests that his absolute faith in the unwillingness of capitalists to destroy property created a fatal 'blind spot in his mentality'.

Although Brennan-Whitmore was later to become good friends with Michael Collins, and serve on his intelligence staff during the war of independence, he was not immediately impressed. Finding him 'silent to the point of surliness', he none the less recognised 'his obvious vigour and youthful energy'. Before the start of the fighting, Brennan-Whitmore also got to meet the young 'Captain de Valera' at Great Brunswick Street. Here he is clearly influenced by later events, and he describes him as dour, aloof and unfriendly, even noting something 'unIrish and foreign' about him. 'We are going to have trouble with that officer' he claimed to have told Sean MacDonagh at the time, after de Valera annoyed him by insisting that every order was signed, countersigned, timed and dated. 'Oh, he's all right,' replied MacDonagh. 'A bit of a stickler for the book of rules. But he is all right.'

Another future Fianna Fáiler (or 'one of Destiny's spoiled children' in Brennan-Whitmore's words) emerges with even less credit. Sean T. O'Kelly is mocked for arriving at the GPO on the afternoon of Easter Monday wearing a perfectly fitting light grey suit, a straw hat with a multicoloured band, a stylish tie, and a light walking cane, and for presenting 'a perfect picture of a young man about town'. Disputing the accounts that O'Kelly had taken a major role in the rebellion, he asserted that O'Kelly had only spent ten minutes in the GPO before announcing, 'And now I will go home to my tea!' never to return. While ostensibly refusing to criticise a man for 'funking a hopeless fight such as ours', Brennan-Whitmore made sure to criticise O'Kelly's later work as an ambassador in Paris ('and an expensive one at that'), and feigns amazement that he ended up as president of Ireland.

There are some nice vignettes of life in Dublin during the fighting. The issue of looting is discussed, which it seems was triggered by a group of boys who broke into a toy shop on O'Connell Street at the start of the week and stole a box of fireworks which were ignited in the centre of the street. By the end of the week Dublin was in flames. Brennan-Whitmore's description is evocative and memorable, and is the most powerful section of the memoir: 'I stood on the rooftops in the gathering gloom. Dublin burning! What a sight! Gruesome, awe-inspiring. Man's inhumanity to man—there is nothing so brutal and callous in all creation.'

As we approach the centenary of the 1916 Rising, and debate its meaning, and the reality, we also need to reflect on the ideals of the Republic which were enunciated then, and our failure to realise them. To gain an insight into what really happened, and the men and women who fought in the rebellion, we should begin with this first-hand account of one of the key participants. There is perhaps no better way of understanding the imagination of an insurrection.

Dr Patrick M. Geoghegan is Associate Professor of History at Trinity College Dublin and Dean of Undergraduate Studies for the university. He presents the award-winning *Talking History* on Newstalk radio.

Introduction

This memoir of the 1916 Rising was completed in 1961, five years before the fiftieth anniversary commemorations of the rebellion. When it was submitted for publication to one leading Irish publisher, it produced *inter alia* the response that some of the content was too controversial. While the negative reply was probably as much a reflection of the deluge of material then appearing on the subject, it is indicative of how much Ireland has changed in the meantime that it is difficult now to find what was judged controversial. Even more indicative of the changing times is the fact that an attempt by the Pearse museum to organise a commemorative conference to mark the seventy-fifth anniversary of the Rising in 1991 had to be abandoned because of lack of official support.[1]

Five years on, we have entered a post-revisionist age in which those who would interpret or re-interpret the Rising might best go back to the evidence of those who were there. *Dublin Burning* is a gripping, first-hand account. It is more than simply an eye-witness account—it is a detailed memoir by a leading participant. Commandant Brennan-Whitmore was not one of the core group who planned and led the rebellion—if he had been it is not likely that he would have escaped the executions which followed. However, he was closely associated with that group and he played a significant role in the Rising. He was a general staff officer in the GPO before taking command of a

Leabharlanna Poibli Chathair Bhaile Átha Cliath
Dublin City Public Libraries

small outpost at North Earl Street. After the Rising, he was one
of the few surviving commandants.

Brennan-Whitmore published a short account of his involvement in the Rising in *An tÓglach* in January and February 1926
as part of a series of memoirs by participants. This early version
focussed on the military aspects of the Rising. A revised and
extended account, with some new material and minor corrections,
was serialised in the *Irish Weekly Independent* in August–
September 1953.[2] The version published here was completed in
1961. It contains some changes, especially in the area of personal
details, and a few corrections, but is closely based on the 1953
account. The manuscript has been reproduced largely without
amendment except for the removal of clear repetition and the
correction of obvious typing errors and misspellings.

The publication of a memoir almost twenty years after the
death of its author and eighty years after the events which it
describes is unusual. It may well be the last memoir by a
participant in the Rising to be published. There have been many
previous accounts by eye-witnesses and participants but few if
any of them evoke so vividly the experience of being there.[3]

William James Brennan-Whitmore was born in Wexford in
1886. Both his parents died when he was a child and he was
raised by his mother's brother James Brennan and his wife
Biddy on a farm at Clonee, Ferns. He later adopted the name
Brennan-Whitmore in honour of his foster parents to whom he
was closely attached. He received his formal education at the
local national school and then spent a short but unhappy
period as a grocer's apprentice in Dublin. Brennan-Whitmore
hoped to follow in his father's footsteps—Thomas Whitmore
had been a journalist with *The People* newspapers in Wexford.

To further this ambition he joined the Royal Irish Regiment in the hope that a spell abroad would enhance his prospects. He served in India in the medical corps and attained the rank of sergeant before leaving the army in 1907.

This army service had a significant impact on Brennan-Whitmore's development in a number of ways, some of them unexpected. Although his uncle was reputedly a Fenian sympathiser, Brennan-Whitmore always insisted that he learned his nationalism from an Irish missionary priest, Fr John Mullan, in the foothills of the Himalayas. When he returned to Wexford, he quickly involved himself in the nationalist movement. He found work as a journalist and freelance writer and joined Arthur Griffith's new Sinn Féin movement and the Gaelic League. He was a Sinn Féin delegate and a Gaelic League branch delegate from 1910 to 1913 when he joined the Volunteers.

Brennan-Whitmore's military background proved useful when he threw himself into the organisation of the Volunteer movement in the south-east. He became officer commanding of the Ferns Company at its inception and, in 1914, adjutant of the North Wexford Brigade. It was also his military background which propelled him from the local to the national stage in 1916. His skill and efficiency in Wexford did not go unnoticed. As he recounts below, he struck up a close personal relationship with J. J. (Ginger) O'Connell, one of the national organisers of the Volunteers, and it was O'Connell who introduced him to the national leadership of the Volunteers.

Before long, Brennan-Whitmore was invited to attend meetings of the military council of the Irish Volunteers. It is clear that he was then, as he remained all his life, a man of strong views. He was a strong advocate of the need to arm and

train the Volunteers properly. Less predictably, he was convinced
that the Volunteers should not seek to replicate British army
structures and tactics. Rather they should adapt to suit Irish
terrain and conditions. As he admits himself, the constant reit-
eration of these views led to his being seen in certain quarters as
something of a nuisance. He was invited to write a training
manual embodying his ideas, which he duly did. Although it
was never published it led to his being appointed to the general
staff of the Volunteers.

The Volunteers were only one of a number of groups who
contributed to the rebellion. Above all, the Rising was engin-
eered by the Irish Republican Brotherhood. Brennan-Whitmore
was not a member of the IRB and, unlike some other Volunteer
officers, he was not invited to join shortly before the Rising.[4]
Like many of his contemporaries, including Eamon de Valera,
he disapproved of oath-bound secret societies and felt the
Volunteers would only succeed if they were an open, public
movement. We have in this memoir a remarkable confirmation
of the often-repeated assertion that the reference to it in the
opening paragraphs of the Proclamation of the Republic was
the first indication for many Volunteers of the existence of the
IRB. In a small room at Liberty Hall on the morning of the
Rising, Brennan-Whitmore sighted the Proclamation lying on a
table and learned for the first time of the role of the under-
ground movement.

Presumably it was his military expertise which persuaded the
Volunteer leadership to discount the obvious disadvantages in
giving a senior position to someone who was unfamiliar with
the local terrain and with the men under his command.
Brennan-Whitmore did not take up his appointment on the

general staff until he received a mobilisation order signed by Thomas MacDonagh on the Wednesday evening before the rebellion was due to start. His story illustrates graphically the confused and desperate nature of the adventure on which the rebels were about to embark. Arriving in Dublin, he had to seek directions from a policeman to the house of his commanding officer. Later, after the seizure of the GPO, when he was ordered by Connolly to occupy and fortify buildings on North Earl Street (across the road from the GPO), he had to enquire where it was. Then, in the final stages, with his command in flames, his attempt to lead his men to safety was hampered by the fact that he was not familiar with the north inner city and the line of retreat to Fairview.

Brennan-Whitmore's view of the Rising is that of a soldier and a journalist. He gives considerable space to the discussion of the military tactics adopted. Although he is admirably loyal to the comrades with whom he endured so much, it is clear that he had reservations about both the long- and short-term preparations for the rebellion. These views are not mainly a product of hindsight—the views expressed in this memoir are consistent with his position before 1916. He was not an advocate of the blood sacrifice—he did believe that a rebellion was a viable military option. The rebellion in Dublin was to be a prelude to a countrywide rising for which it would buy time.[5]

Although he does not say so, Brennan-Whitmore would have been more at home fighting on his home ground in Wexford. Nonetheless he acquitted himself with some distinction in the different surroundings in which he found himself. Both in the GPO and later, in his North Earl Street command post, he displayed competence and clear-sightedness. His knowledge of fortifications certainly contributed to the low casualty rate suffered by his command and perhaps even in the GPO itself. Had the British attacked from Amiens Street as Connolly expected, they would have met stout resistance. In the event, and much to Connolly's surprise but not to Brennan-Whitmore's, the assault when it came was by way of bombardment, against which there was no real means of defence.

One of the features of Brennan-Whitmore's narrative is the series of pen pictures which he draws of the main leaders. The portraits are loyal, generous and revealing. His admiration for MacDonagh, Clarke and MacDermott is evident. Nowhere is there a more moving description of the physical condition of Joseph Plunkett on the eve of the Rising. He was clearly impressed with Pearse's idealism if not by his military acumen. Michael Collins, who was later to become one of Brennan-Whitmore's heroes, does not loom large here although they came in close contact at the start of the Rising. In contrast, his assessment of Arthur Griffith is more forthcoming: Brennan-Whitmore was deeply influenced by many of Griffith's ideas.

While he did not share Connolly's social vision and found his view that capitalists would not bombard property owned by their fellow capitalists extremely naïve, Brennan-Whitmore admired his ability and leadership. Given that he was a deeply committed Catholic and a social conservative who had little sympathy for notions of class conflict, it is ironic that he found himself working directly under Connolly and in charge of a group which was comprised mainly of Connolly's followers.

A feature of many of the accounts of 1916 written by participants is an element of setting-the-record-straight and sometimes even score-settling.[6] Brennan-Whitmore is more inclined to the former than the latter. By and large he gives due credit to people who were later to be on the opposite side of the Treaty divide, even if he cannot resist mild side-swipes at de Valera and Seán T. O'Kelly. As befits a soldier, he is generous too about his military adversaries and has no great complaints about the treatment of his men after their arrest. The only real venom is directed against politicians, particularly the members of the Irish Parliamentary Party.[7]

The story of the 1916 Rising is well known but Brennan-Whitmore has a journalist's eye for detail which gives his memoir an immediacy and a human dimension which is lacking in many other accounts. Brennan-Whitmore records the puzzled response of the population of Dublin to the events unfolding in their city, their impatience, frustration and humour, the problems posed by looting and the firm but pragmatic response of his garrison. There are tales of bravery and idealism as well as the absurd and bizarre—drunken looters, residents unwilling to be moved to safety, an insurgent who has to be excused from his post to return a set of keys so that his workplace might be opened after the holiday break, a publican who offers the contents of his pub for the cause. The mundane personal details, the confusion, the uncertainty and the human frailty are all caught in a way which allows the Rising to be seen as a real event rather than as an abstraction.

After the Rising, Brennan-Whitmore was imprisoned in Frongoch in north Wales where he was elected camp adjutant. He prepared and secretly delivered a series of lectures to senior officers on the application of general principles of military strategy and tactics to the Irish terrain. On his release he returned to Wexford where he resumed his work as a journalist and wrote his well-known account of his imprisonment, *With the Irish in Frongoch*, published in December 1917.[8] He remained active in the nationalist movement, working as an intelligence officer on Collins's staff and contributing articles to the IRA newspaper, *An tÓglach*. He married Anna Josephine Murphy of Ferns in 1920.

Brennan-Whitmore took the pro-Treaty side in 1922 and joined the national army with the rank of commandant. He was based at army headquarters as a staff officer and worked for army intelligence. He succeeded Piaras Béaslaí as editor of *An tÓglach*, the official army journal. In 1926, he published the first army list and directory of the Irish army.[9] The following year, he retired from the army and returned to Wexford where he took up farming. Later, he founded and edited a local newspaper, *The Record*, in Gorey and ran a printing business. He maintained a lively interest in national and international affairs, becoming an inveterate speaker and writer of letters to the newspapers.

If anything, the distrust of politicians which is evident in *Dublin Burning* intensified with age as he became disillusioned with the failure of the new state, particularly under de Valera. He was an advocate of national government during the Second World War. Perhaps surprisingly, he supported Clann na Poblachta for a time after its establishment, in the hope that it would pursue financial reform and break the link with sterling. He died in 1977.

Pauric Travers
St Patrick's College
Drumcondra
1996

Ante-Scriptum

An explanation is due to the reader as to how it came to pass that I, a resident of County Wexford and an officer of the Irish Volunteers in that historic county, came to be fighting in Dublin during the Easter Rising instead of being with my own comrades. This is a question which has been frequently put to me.

The Ferns Company of the Irish Volunteers was one of the earliest corps to be formed in the country. I was its founder and commanding officer; and later I was appointed adjutant to the North Wexford Brigade.[10]

Shortly after the formation of the Ferns Company, Captain J. J. O'Connell, MA, chief organiser GHQ, came on a tour of inspection. 'Ginger' O'Connell (as he was affectionately called) had served in the United States army. Towards the end of 1913 or very early in 1914 Sean MacDermott, a prominent member of the Irish Republican Brotherhood (IRB) who was executed for his part in the Easter Rising, met O'Connell in New York and persuaded him to return to Ireland to help in organising and training the Volunteers. After the inspection, O'Connell and myself had a long private conversation. We found that our views on the form of organisation and methods of training coincided almost exactly. These views differed radically from those being used at the time. This unison of ideas led to a close personal friendship which lasted until his untimely and lamented death. He had risen to the rank of lieutenant general and chief of staff of the Free State army; and it was his arrest by irregulars which finally precipitated our deplorable civil war.[11]

In the early days of the Volunteers, ex- and reserve members of the British army were used as organisers and instructors, and in many cases were appointed to the command of Volunteer corps. The Volunteers were, in consequence, being organised on the model and trained in the methods of the British army. It was to this outcome that O'Connell and myself strongly objected. We had no animus to the people themselves.

Due almost entirely to O'Connell's influence and partly to the advanced nature of the training and equipment of the North Wexford Volunteers, I was occasionally invited to attend meetings in Dublin of the military council. This body was the real power behind the Volunteers and was composed, I believe, almost entirely of leading members of the IRB. I was not a member of this council; nor was I ever a member of the IRB.

On these rare occasions I pressed my views very strongly, pointing out that we could not possibly withstand the British army, in the event of a clash, if organised and trained on their model; that all the reservists would be called up on the outbreak of war, which was then obviously imminent; that practically all the ex-members would again join the colours; and that as a result the Volunteer organisation would be thrown into a state of confusion at a most critical period. My views were received so unsympathetically as to almost amount to indifference. At the time I could not understand this indifference to a vitally important factor in our situation, but later I was to understand it very thoroughly.

About the time of the outbreak of the First World War, James Connolly, leader of the Irish Citizen Army and organised trade unionism, told Cathal O'Shannon, a veteran nationalist and journalist from Belfast, that he wished to get in touch with the IRB and, if necessary, was prepared to take the oath of that body for the purpose of establishing friendly relations between militant nationalism and Irish labour.[12] Up to that time relations between militant nationalism and the Citizen Army were strained due to the unwarranted belligerency of Sean O'Casey, the playwright, and his personal animosity to Countess Markievicz. I was always given to understand that O'Casey was a member of the IRB, but whether he was or not he certainly shirked the Rising and later removed himself to England to live.[13]

James Connolly then began to attend at least some of the meetings of the military council and it was here we met for the first time. We clashed almost at once. His idea of a stand-up fight against the British army in Dublin was totally opposed to that of O'Connell and myself. Incredible as it may now appear, Connolly was firmly convinced that the British army would never use artillery fire in Dublin against entrenched 'rebels'. James Connolly was a well-read and highly intelligent as well as a very determined man. His repeated retort to objections against this idea of his was always the same: 'Capitalists will never destroy capitalist property.'

In the end, Connolly's plan prevailed. In main outline it was much the same as that which he had proposed to Arthur Griffith, when they were both members of the Irish Transvaal Committee during the Boer War, and which Griffith promptly rejected because it was not practical.[14] In the meantime conditions had changed very materially but Connolly's plan remained largely unchanged.[15]

Towards the end, I am afraid, I came to be regarded as a bit of a nuisance. At one of the meetings of the council, which was held in Parnell Square and more or less disguised as a meeting of the Gaelic League, one of those present, I think it was Eamonn Ceannt, somewhat brusquely said I should write a textbook for the Volunteers embodying my ideas. That was a challenge which could not be baulked. At the end of the meeting Bulmer Hobson, secretary to the executive council of the Volunteers and an important member of the IRB, J. J. O'Connell and myself remained on after the others had departed. I recollect Hobson remarking with pardonable irritation: 'They talk of setting the heather afire! The heather is a blasted bog!'

Much has been written about the 'arrest' of Bulmer Hobson on the eve of the Rising. This use of the word 'arrest' is a grave and unmerited reflection on Hobson who was a sincere and loyal Irishman. He differed, as many of us did, as to when and under what circumstances a rising should be precipitated. He held his views strongly and the responsibility of his position in the movement entitled him, if he thought it necessary, to give public expression to his views. It was to avoid the possibility of any such premature pronouncement that he was placed under temporary restraint. None of his colleagues, I feel sure, doubted his sincerity or loyalty.

As we came away from the meeting together, O'Connell pressed me to lose no time in getting to work on the textbook, offering at the same time to give me all the help I might require. I promised to begin the work as soon as I got back to Wexford. This I did, basing the textbook partly on the successful tactics employed by Father Murphy in the Wexford Rising of 1798 and partly on those of de Wett of Boer War fame.

The Ferns Company had purchased some German Mauser rifles and ammunition from a firm of traders (Lawler) in Fownes Street, Dublin. We used up the ammunition at target practice in Kilbora wood where we had set up a rifle range. We were then informed by GHQ that they could not give us any ammunition for our now useless Mausers and they offered to exchange American single-barrel shotguns for them. I was not enamoured of the suggestion; but even shotguns were better than no guns at all, so the exchange was agreed to. For this purpose a Ford sedan motor car, the property of Father Michael Murphy of Ferns, was borrowed and I availed of this transport to send my manuscript and drawings to GHQ. The exchange was safely effected, but on the return journey, in Grafton Street, the car was halted by detectives and searched. The shotguns were discovered and the two Volunteers, Lieutenant Patrick Doyle and Vol. Pender, were taken into custody and later sentenced to prison. They were in jail when the Rising took place.

The manuscript and drawings were, however, safely delivered and shortly afterwards I was informed it had been accepted for publication as a textbook for the Volunteers. As a matter of fact it was never published.[16] It was due partly to this textbook but mainly, I believe, to the personal influence of J. J. O'Connell that I was eventually appointed to the general staff of the Irish Volunteers. For obvious reasons I could not take up this appointment at once. Apart from private matters, the plans for the participation of the Wexford men in the Rising had to be finally hammered out, and commands and local corps appointments had to be handed over. However, late on the Wednesday evening preceding Easter I received a mobilisation order, signed by Comdt General Thomas MacDonagh, directing me to report without undue delay to the chief of staff. I travelled to Dublin on Good Friday by the evening mail train.

That, in brief outline, is the explanation.

Chapter 1
Eve of the Rising

O n Good Friday afternoon I walked from my home in Clonee to the railway station at Ferns, a distance of three and a half miles. I was dressed in my best navy suit, with a soft felt hat cocked on the side of my head, a light raincoat on my left arm and a light walking cane. I carried no weapons or documents of any sort. It would be rather difficult for any casual observer to see in me an Irish rebel setting out on a desperate adventure, which I was well aware would end in failure.

Camolin station would have suited me better but unfortunately the evening mail train did not stop there. I made some calls in the village to bid *bonjour* to comrades whose occupations were either in the little village or convenient to it. I passed the police barracks on my way.

On arriving at the platform I was surprised to note that no police patrol was in evidence. At that time the movements of the Irish Volunteers were under the constant surveillance of the Royal Irish Constabulary (RIC). I went into the station and bought a return ticket to Dublin. The purpose of this was to give the inevitable enquirer the impression that I was coming back after the weekend.

Just before the train steamed into the station two RIC men appeared on the road bridge which spanned the railway. One of them raised his hand in salute and then gave me a friendly wave of it. They were sly rogues the same RIC. Not to be outdone, in an appearance of goodwill I raised my hat and waved back enthusiastically. At the same time I knew quite well that as soon as the train left they would saunter into the station master's office and learn that I had gone to Dublin and had purchased a return ticket.[17]

But I had no intention of going into the city terminus at Westland Row. Ranelagh was a braking stop. All passenger trains to the city made a momentary stop at Ranelagh for the purpose of reducing speed and preventing the train overrunning the buffers at the terminus, as had happened some time before.

A quick glance up and down the platform assured me that there was no police patrol present. I left the train, hastened down the steps, took a tram into the city and booked into the Royal Exchange Hotel, Parliament Street. This was a favourite resort for country members of the Volunteers.

Having to report my arrival to Comdt General Thomas MacDonagh, and as my knowledge of Dublin was limited to the principal streets, I had to enquire from the hall porter which tram would take me out to Rathmines. My destination was a house in Oakley Road in that district. The kindly tram conductor set me down at the proper corner. What a wonderful knowledge of the side streets and roads along their routes these old tram conductors had and how unfailingly courteous and helpful they were.[18]

At the corner of Oakley Road my troubles really began. It was a typical suburban road of private houses, with the usual small garden in front. I did not know how the house numbers ran. Some distance down the road a large metropolitan policeman stood immobile under a road lamp. It was obvious that his job was to keep a close watch on MacDonagh's house. But which house was it?

Nearly all the houses appeared to be in complete darkness and it was impossible to read the house numbers from the pathway. To have opened a gate at random, gone up the path, read the number, returned to the road and begun counting as I walked along would have looked ridiculous. Going straight up to the policeman I asked him, in the best imitation of an English accent I could manage, if he would kindly direct me to the residence of Professor Thomas MacDonagh, who was on the staff of University College, Dublin.[19]

He pointed to a house on the opposite side and then gratuitously added that he did not think there was anybody at home. I thanked him and added that I was an English friend of the professor's over on an unexpected visit. I said it was quite possible at that hour, as I was not expected, that everybody was out, and if so, I would call again in the morning.

It took several rings on the door bell before there was any answer; even then the light was not switched on in the hall and the door was only opened on the chain. Through the gloom of this opening a bald head showed up whitely and a terse voice demanded to know what I wanted. In a low tone of voice I gave my name and rank, stating that I had an appointment with the professor. I added that I had just arrived from Wexford. The voice, still very terse and brusque, said simply that the professor was not at home. I said that I had booked into the Royal Exchange Hotel and could be contacted there. I then withdrew.

Meanwhile the large policeman had moved over to my side of the road but made no approach to this particular house. When

I again thanked him for his help he asked me if anybody was at home. It was plain my ring had been answered so I said, only a maid. One thing was clear, the professor was already partly, at least, on 'his keeping'.

Expecting a message I sat up late that night chatting with other guests but none came. As Easter Saturday morning slowly wore away and still no message came, I began to feel uneasy. It was getting dangerously close to what I believed was the vital hour and I was naturally anxious to make contact. My difficulty was that I knew very few of the leading Volunteers in the city and of those I did know, I did not know their habitats. I began to fear I would be left stranded. Moreover, there seemed to be a bit of a mix up as the mobilisation order had been signed by MacDonagh and not Joseph Mary Plunkett, whose staff I was originally appointed to. I did not know at the time that Plunkett was seriously ill.

However, late in the afternoon, by which time I had begun to despair and was considering what steps I could take to make contact, a message arrived to the effect that I was to report to MacDonagh at Liberty Hall the following morning. Whilst this relieved my mind somewhat, it still left a degree of confusion. Liberty Hall was not a Volunteers headquarters, but that of the Citizen Army, as well as the Irish Transport and General Workers Union. I was aware that a *rapprochement* had taken place between the Citizen Army and the Irish Volunteers, but as far as I knew they were still two distinct and independent bodies. Nor did I feel too happy at being directed to the stronghold of James Connolly, with whose ideas concerning a rising I had clashed.

But the Sunday morning newspapers contained a veritable bombshell. They carried Professor Eoin MacNeill's startling order of the day. The professor was president of the Volunteer executive and chief of staff, but in respect of the latter position only in title. The order itself was both drastic and peremptory. It ran:

April 22, 1916.

Owing to the very critical position, all orders given to Irish Volunteers for tomorrow, Easter Sunday, are hereby rescinded, and no parades, marches, or other movements of Irish Volunteers will take place. Each individual Volunteer will obey this order strictly in every particular.

Eoin MacNeill,
Chief of Staff,
Irish Volunteers.

MacNeill had learned, late on Saturday evening, that the IRB leaders and Connolly intended to turn the Easter parade into a rising as had been originally intended, and that this was to be done without the concurrence of all the executive as a body. MacNeill at once rushed his order of the day to the newspapers and sent couriers (including the only other general staff officer, Capt J. J. O'Connell) hot haste to the country commands. I have always entertained a great respect and admiration for Professor MacNeill in the rather invidious position in which he was placed.

When the Irish Volunteers were in the process of planning a rising, its IRB promoters knew quite well that, despite the very excellent excuse for such a move which bigoted Orangemen had so amply and completely afforded them, they dare not let any appearance of their control leak out to the traditional enemy. If they had done so, the Irish Volunteers would have received short shrift from Dublin Castle.

The British authorities had smilingly connived at the open organisation of the Irish Citizen Army—its drilling, marching in military formation, and the carrying out of its 'manoeuvres'—only because a British intelligence officer had set in train the march of events which led to that body's establishment. Moreover, this official connivance was due to their ultimate purpose—drafting this army practically holus-bolus into the British army as cannon fodder in the world war. But the plan had gone awry and the functionaries—especially the permanent under secretary, Sir Matthew Nathan, a German Jew—were smarting under a sense of defeat and frustration. How joyously they would have leaped to the work of suppression if any suspicion had leaked out that the driving force was the IRB.[20]

Hence, the executive of the IRB looked around for a public figure to head the Volunteers. They found him in the person of Eoin MacNeill, who was really 'tailor made', so to speak, for their purpose: a man of unblemished personal character, a profound scholar, a sincere patriot, and, at the same time, a humble man and a gentleman. A better choice could not possibly have been made.

Unfortunately (perhaps it was really a blessing) MacNeill suffered the defects of a sterling character. He deeply and sincerely believed he was what he had been elected to be, the head and supreme authority of the Irish Volunteers. In reality, however, he was regarded by the heads of the IRB as a 'figurehead leader' whose authority would cease at the vital moment.[21]

Equally, the IRB leadership were at fault. Knowing, as they undoubtedly did, the true character of MacNeill and what his reaction would be under certain circumstances, they should have made plans to counteract that reaction. They did not do so. The result in Easter week was simply chaos throughout the whole organisation.

Receipt of the order caused massive confusion in the whole country Volunteer organisation. Its ultimate effect was to isolate the country corps from the city and, with the exceptions of Wexford and Galway, immobilise them.

The opening phrase of the order—owing to the very critical position—was an unfortunate choice. Actually it referred to the differences that had existed in the executive as to when and what circumstances were best for a successful rising. This, in itself, was bad enough but the phrase set off a whole series of wildcat rumours.

Practically everyone in the city who knew anything about nationalist affairs was aware, for days ahead, that the Volunteers and Citizen Army had planned a full-muster parade through the principal streets for Easter Sunday. It was the first time since the great public funeral of the old Fenian, O'Donovan Rossa, that such a parade was to be carried out and most people had looked forward to it with pleasant anticipation, for Dublin dearly loves a free public spectacle. What few indeed knew, or even guessed, was that on this parade the Volunteers and Citizen Army would be marching directly on predetermined strategic and tactical points in the metropolis, which they would seize by surprise and thus begin the rising. The element of surprise was regarded as crucial for initial success. To lull officialdom, many marches and mock 'manoeuvres' had been held in the city from time to time without any untoward event and this particular parade was rumoured to be merely 'a show of strength'.

The disturbed state of my mind caused by Easter Sunday morning's announcement can be better imagined than described. I was aware that every member of the executive anticipated an eventual rising and was agreed on it, at least, to this extent: if the British authorities attempted to disarm the Volunteers they should fight no matter what the consequences. All were agreed on that course. Failing such an attempt being made some members were against initiating a rising unless supported by considerable aid in the form of arms and ammunition from America or Germany or both.

A majority of the IRB members were in favour of a rising irrespective of whether promised aid came or not. Their firm conviction was that 'a blood sacrifice' was absolutely necessary for the redemption of Ireland. They were convinced and sincere in this belief: with them, it amounted to an article of nationalist faith. Their right, however, to demand a blood sacrifice from their innocent followers could well be called into question on moral and other grounds.[22]

The IRB members, despite the fact that they were poets and dreamers of beautiful dreams—or because they were such— were definitely the most determined and decisive characters on the executive, and they had a powerful ally in Connolly when he was sworn in. Indeed, it is no exaggeration to say that they were the great driving force behind the Irish Volunteers movement. Each and every one of them would have been happy to face a martyr's death in the cause of a free and independent Irish nation.

But Eoin MacNeill, whilst every bit as earnest as any of the IRB and as patriotic and ready to make sacrifice, was also a more clear-sighted humanitarian. Whilst Pearse and the other IRB men might even welcome the prospect of a martyr's death for Ireland in the hope that great national advantage might flow from it and whilst Connolly might be happy to seal his socialist faith with his blood, MacNeill was of a totally different outlook. He put first the rank and file and the anguish and desolation that would inevitably flow from military failure.

Realising these differences, Pearse sought to make amends to MacNeill when he said: 'Let no man point the finger of scorn at Eoin MacNeill.' It was a generous attempt at the *amende honorable*.

Then, on the eve of the planned rising, a series of unhappy events occurred. True to its promise the German government, then at war with Great Britain and its allies, despatched a shipload of badly needed arms and ammunition to the Volunteers. This was entirely due to the efforts of Sir Roger Casement. By prior arrangement, the *Aud* left Lübeck on 9 April. But largely owing to domestic differences the Volunteer executive did not want the cargo of arms to be landed before 23 April. As the *Aud* carried no wireless, the German government could not contact it at sea. This *faux pas* was entirely due to poor planning on the part of the executive.

In due course the *Aud* arrived off Tralee Bay and remained there for nearly twenty-four hours, sending out signals to the coast. Owing to the carelessness or inefficiency of the officer commanding the Volunteers in that area, there were neither patrols nor lookouts maintained. Eventually the *Aud* was sighted by a British naval craft, which signalled it to follow into harbour. Not being a war vessel the *Aud* had no option but to comply. However, the gallant captain and crew managed to sink the ship and its cargo. This loss was a heavy blow.[23]

It was by no means the only heavy blow at this critical moment. Sir Roger Casement, who had come ashore from a German submarine, was captured by an RIC patrol in the same Kerry area. And three technicians, who were sent down to Kerry to seize the cable and wireless station at Valentia, took a wrong turning and were drowned, with only the driver of the motor car miraculously escaping. It looked as if even fate was against us; and needless to say these unhappy occurrences in no way lessened the degree of tension that already existed in the executive. Worse still, they alerted the British to the seriousness of the menace posed by the Irish Volunteers.

The leadership of the Kerry Volunteers in this area, which had been fully advised of dates and events, deserves the severest censure. Nor can the executive escape blame for the drowning: it should have ensured that the driver of the motor car had a good ordnance survey roadmap and was able to read it. It will be argued that such criticism is easy after the events. It is not intended as criticism so much as underlining the inadequacy of the training and knowledge of the personnel in positions of local leadership.

But the real torment in my mind was: is our effort going to be as futile as those of Robert Emmet and the Fenians? So far we had been able to arm openly and to train to a certain extent. We were, moreover, able to do so throughout the thirty-two counties, for there were organised Volunteer corps in the Ulster counties as well as everywhere else. No such opportunity had occurred since Grattan's time in 1779. It certainly looked on the face of it as if history was going to repeat itself.

To return to MacNeill's order of the day: many people read into the phrase 'owing to the very critical position' a reference to a British plan for the military occupation of Dublin. Such a move by Dublin Castle would have hamstrung both the Volunteers and the Citizen Army.

In March 1916, P. J. Little, editor of *New Ireland*, the official organ of the Redmondite Volunteers, told an Irish Volunteer officer he was getting, from a friendly official in Dublin Castle, particulars of a document in code setting out a plan for the military occupation of the city. This titbit of news naturally spread around. Eventually when a copy was received Alderman Tom Kelly read it at a meeting of Dublin Corporation. It caused a first-class sensation.

At first, publication of the document in the press was prohibited by the British censor; then later, when the ban was lifted, the document was described officially as 'a pure fabrication'. There is a very wise old maxim to the effect that no rumour is to be taken as true until it is officially denied. In any case it can be taken as certain that the working out of such a plan was, in the circumstances, merely a matter of routine British general staff work.

Eoin MacNeill was reported as saying, when he read it: 'The Lord has delivered them into our hands.' But this was delightfully vague as to precisely what use he intended to make of this gift from the good Lord. Pearse was much more forthright and explicit. He was reported as saying 'it is a race between us and the [British] government'. Certainly the document strengthened the hands of those who believed in a blood sacrifice. They had, so to speak, received the green light and only the necessity of securing an adequate supply of arms stayed their hand. Now that hope was lost.

There are those who assert that the 'leaking' of this document was deliberate and had as its object the provoking of a premature rising. If this were true, why the rigid censorship of publication? Presumably officialdom would welcome the fullest publicity. Furthermore, the completeness with which the British authorities were taken by surprise and the slowness of the British military in seeking to come to grips with the entrenched Volunteers and Citizen Army go a long way to disprove this theory. It was a theory that rose out of our past history.[24]

However all this may be, the plan, as published, read as follows:

Secret

The following precautionary measures have been sanctioned by the Irish Office on the recommendation of the G.O.C. the Forces in Ireland. All preparations to put these measures in force immediately on receipt of an Order from the Chief Secretary's Office, Dublin Castle and signed by the Under Secretary and the G.O.C. the Forces in Ireland.

First: the following persons are to be placed under arrest: All members of Sinn Fein; the Central Executive of the Irish Sinn Fein Volunteers; General Council Irish Sinn Fein Volunteers; County Board Sinn Fein Volunteers; Executive Committee National Volunteers; Coisde Gaelic League.

See lists A3 and 4 and supplementary list A2.

Metropolitan police and Royal Irish Constabulary forces in Dublin city will be confined to barracks under the direction of the competent Military Authority. An order will be issued to inhabitants of the city to remain in their houses until such times as the competent Military Authority may otherwise direct or permit. Pickets chosen from units of Territorial

Forces will be placed at all points marked on Maps 3 and 4. Accompanying mounted patrols will continuously visit all points and report every hour.

The following premises will be occupied by adequate forces, and all necessary measures taken without reference to Headquarters.

First: known as Liberty Hall, Beresford Place; No. 6 Harcourt Street, Sinn Fein Building; No. 2 Dawson Street, Headquarters Sinn Fein Volunteers; No. 12 D'Olier Street, *Nationality* Office; No. 41 Rutland Square, Forresters' Hall; Sinn Fein Volunteers premises in the city; all National Volunteer premises in the city; Trades Council premises, Capel Street; Surrey House, Leinster Road, Rathmines.

The following premises will be isolated and all communication to or from prevented: premises known as Archbishop's House, Drumcondra; Mansion House, Dawson Street; No. 40 Herbert Park; Larkfield, Kimmage Road; Woodtown Park, Ballyboden; St. Enda's College, Hermitage, Rathfarnham; and in addition premises in List D, see Maps 3 and 4.

This order, in effect, meant a clean sweep. If it were merely a 'nudge' to premature action, it was certainly a most complete and thorough 'nudge'.[25]

The uncertainties of all these events caused a high degree of tension in nationalist circles though little of it was apparent in the outward appearance and behaviour of those most vitally concerned. There was an overreadiness to laugh and joke and a wonderfully simulated air of confidence.

In British official and Unionist circles it was no less a period of strain and difficulty. The European war was going very badly for Great Britain and her allies. Due directly to inflammatory speeches made by leaders of the British Conservative Party, the successfully accomplished rebellion of the Orangemen in the north-east and the alleged mutiny of the British forces stationed on the Curragh had produced a situation in Ireland well calculated to unnerve the ablest and most experienced states-men. Those then in charge of the destinies of both Great Britain and Ireland were far removed from either category. No less than five separate armed forces were marching in Ireland: the British forces, the armed RIC, the Irish Volunteers and Citizen Army, the Redmondite Volunteers, and the Orangemen's army. Never in the long history of Ireland had the internal situation been more confused and explosive.

Chapter 2
Plans for the Rising

It always seemed to me that the plans for a rising against the British occupation of Ireland were originally groups of ideas rather than one coherent plan worked out on strictly military lines by a military staff. Such plans, whether for activation by a regular or irregular force, involved a number of technical details which could only be efficiently dealt with by a military staff devoted to a particular aspect and not burdened with any other facets of the situation.

I came away from the few meetings of the military council which I was privileged to attend with a feeling of frustration. I had not much interest in purely political matters, but I did want to know to a reasonable extent the total available manpower, the amount of arms and ammunition that could with some certainty be counted upon, the main strategic and tactical objectives, and the grouping of units for the attainment of these objectives. In addition there were the problems of transportation, which involved problems of timing and co-ordination, as well as commissariat and hospitalisation. Even for a volunteer force all such problems have to be dealt with in advance of actual warfare.

I could never get any real satisfaction on such points except from J. J. O'Connell. This may have been due to the fact that I was not a member of the IRB and the fact that in various public speeches I had made, and in articles I had written, I had laid it down categorically that this movement was going to succeed because there was no secret organisation behind it! At that time I was a very unsophisticated young man. Under such circumstances it was understandable that members should hesitate to open their minds fully to me. However as the critical hour drew near I gained a much fuller picture of the general set-up.

From my experience of these pre-Rising discussions, and from my talks with O'Connell, it became evident that there were two distinct schools of thought in the executive. The first and foremost of these held that a 'blood sacrifice' alone would be needed to rouse the general public from the state of apathy into which it had been lulled by parliamentarianism. All this was simply a matter of ideas. And in this connection it must be borne in mind that a period of almost seventy years had passed since the last military effort to achieve freedom.

This sacrificial group comprised such outstanding figures as Joseph Mary Plunkett, Thomas MacDonagh, Eamonn Ceannt, Thomas Ashe, Sean MacDermott, Thomas J. Clarke, and their head and font was undoubtedly Patrick Pearse. They had a surprisingly large following scattered throughout the country. They were dedicated men. All those, so far as my personal knowledge goes, belonged to the IRB and had that secret organisation solidly behind them.[26]

Their philosophy was built on the old slogan: 'England's difficulty is Ireland's opportunity.' They were determined not to let the present opportunity slip through their hands because England was in greater difficulty than ever before in its history. It is obvious that such men were not fundamentally concerned with a successful outcome of the conflict.

By that I do not mean to suggest that they did not wish and plan for military success. They certainly did. But military success was not their fundamental objective. They knew and understood their history, and the facts of the current situation—that the obstacles to military success were well insurmountable. They believed that through a willing blood sacrifice victory would eventually accrue, not to themselves, but to the nation.

Adherents to the second school of thought were really only prepared to take the initiative in starting the fighting provided that there was a reasonable chance of military success. The ultimate hope of this group was a compromise which would register a considerable advance on the Home Rule Bill as regards both its terms and its immediate implementation. At this period of our history, despite all the brave words spoken and written, the Irish Republic, sovereign and independent, was no more than an ideal.

The second group considered that the building up of the numerical and armed strength was essential to the achievement of this compromise. This line of thought led to the placing of much reliance on outside assistance of a substantial nature. Failing such compromise they were, on this basis of outside assistance, prepared to commit the Volunteers to action. But not otherwise.

Such outside aid was looked for from Germany and the United States. The IRB, owing to its close association with John Devoy's Clann na Gael organisation in America, believed it could secure considerable aid in men, money and arms. And here common ground was found for both schools of thought.

In her excellent book, *Portrait of a Rebel Father*, Norah Connolly O'Brien describes a secret mission on which she was sent by her father, James Connolly, to America. So secret was this mission that she was required to commit her instructions to memory and was not allowed to make any notes concerning it. I had always understood that her journey was in connection with the fund that was to finance the Rising and which was supposed to have been guaranteed by Clann na Gael.

In connection with this alleged fund it may be interesting to note that one day during the actual fighting, whilst making the rounds of our position in North Earl Street, I overheard some men of the Citizen Army discussing our situation. As I came through a hole in the wall, leading from one building to another, I heard one of them, Paddy Swanzy, a baker by trade, say to his companions: 'I don't care if I'm killed. We have been assured there is a fund of £3 million to provide for the dependants of any of us who may be killed.' On making discreet enquiries I found this very generally to be the belief of the men of the Citizen Army who were members of my garrison.

While I knew that finances to some extent had been guaranteed by the Clann it was certainly news to me that a £3 million fund had been promised in respect of casualties. Several years afterwards a retired head constable of the RIC showed me a file, which he declared was a true copy of an official file, and a letter in it purported to record the fact that a Jewish bank in America had financed the Rising to the tune of £3 million.

But personally I am bound to say that I never came across any factual evidence that such a fund existed. I feel convinced that it was one of those incredible rumours that spring up—no one knows how—in times of stress and excitement, and spread far and near with the greatest rapidity. Certainly if such a fund ever did exist some people have a lot of explaining to do.[27]

But this dependence on outside aid went much further and deeper than was generally known at the time. It is, of course, well known that Sir Roger Casement, at the request of the Volunteer executive, had gone to Germany to seek aid. What is not so well known is that Comdt General Joseph Plunkett had spent some months in Germany on a similar mission. Plunkett's international activities however went further afield than Germany. The British empire included many Islamic countries, stretching from India to North Africa, and in all of these there were many potential and actual national revolts. Plunkett had studied these and was, I believe, in touch with Islamic nationalist personnel, chiefly in the Egyptian area.[28]

I have in my possession a book of his dealing with the subject of Islamic and Western civilisations, on the flyleaf of which his signature is inscribed in both Gaelic and Arabic characters. These facts are, I think, very little known. The inevitability of war between England and Germany had been apparent ever since King Edward vii had gone on his 'peace mission' to ring Germany round with enemies. If, on the outbreak of such a war, Islamic nationalists could be induced to revolt, and if the revolt was of a sufficiently widespread nature, the effect on the military outcome of an Irish revolt might well be considerable. All these extensive activities formed an integral part of the general plans for the Rising. If they came to fruition in the hour of need they might well spell the difference between victory and defeat.

Turning to the more direct military plans for the Rising, British military strength in Ireland was concentrated mainly in the metropolis and the great military centre of the Curragh of Kildare. This left the west and south-west of the country more or less weakly held, and as this part was the remotest from England it formed the best area for the contemplated landing of arms and ammunition. And quick distribution was as important as landing.

The basic idea was to seize Dublin by a swift surprise attack and immobilise the British forces not so much by dint of the attack as by threat and manoeuvre, and this strategy of containment by threat applied to the Curragh as well as to Dublin. This, it was confidently expected, would gain the necessary margin of time not only to land the arms and distribute them but also to get the provincial brigades properly in motion.

A further problem was how best to deal with the armed and organised Orangemen in the north-east corner. Many different views were expressed but there was a general feeling that the Orangemen would stick to their own area and leave the problems of relief in the south to the British military. Indeed, some of the Volunteer leaders in this area professed to be in possession of reliable information that such was actually the intention of the Orangemen.

Anyhow, there was a general belief among the executive that severing road and rail communication with the north-east, combined with the threat offered by the Volunteers in that area and the threat of invasion by Volunteers from adjoining counties, would suffice to tie down the Orange and British forces in this particular locality.

Therefore, the main initial objective of the Rising, apart from the seizure of the capital and the containment of the Curragh, was to gain time for the successful landing and distribution of arms and ammunition and for getting our country forces properly distributed and on the move.

Inevitably there would be a certain amount of confusion and misunderstanding amidst the issuing of orders and counter-orders in the first few days, and it was vital to gain time to sort this out and have the country commands tightened up and made militarily effective.

With regard to Dublin city itself, the plan was to seize by surprise attack Dublin Castle, the Telephone Exchange in Crown Alley, the British GHQ at Parkgate and the General Post Office (GPO) in O'Connell Street. These four objectives formed the heart of the plan. If the surprise was complete—and surprise was heavily banked on—it was believed that these main objectives could be seized with very little fighting or casualties.

Meanwhile other units of the Volunteers, Citizen Army and Hibernian Rifles were to occupy and fortify a ring of important and strategic buildings around the centre of the city. No difficulty was anticipated in these seizures. They were to be so strongly fortified as to render them practically impregnable to attack by infantry. These plans for the city had been worked out in great detail and approved by the executive.

At that time the general conception of an uprising in a city was the erection of street barricades and the manning of them by the rebels. In fact the word 'barricades' had become the symbol of city uprisings. In Connolly's view barricades were of secondary importance. His idea was to seize great blocks of buildings, fortify them and then punch holes leading from one set of premises to another within the block, so as to facilitate the massing of men at one threatened point. He did not disdain barricades and in fact provided for them, but he regarded them as secondary in importance.[29]

With the exception of Wexford county I cannot write of personal knowledge of the final plans for the country commands. But the really black spot from our point of view was what is known in military parlance as 'the Waterford entry into Ireland'. This was a convenient port for England and possessed good dock and harbour facilities. A force successfully landed there would quickly reach the centre of Ireland and once there the strategic advantage would pass to it. It could move in any direction: it would nullify our effort to contain the Curragh, with which contact would be quickly made; it would seriously hamper an effective distribution of arms from the west coast; and it would enable a large combined attack to be made on the insurgents in the capital—it being certain that the first place in which the British would seek to suppress the Rising would be Dublin.

Our precise local difficulty was that Waterford was a pro-Redmondite and pro-British stronghold, and the Irish Volunteers were weak there. Any attempt at seizures and occupations would certainly meet with strong opposition from the inhabitants. O'Connell and I had time and again stressed these facts. In our view the only effective form of defence at this vital point would be the erection of strong offensive points to the immediate north of the city with flanking threats to the west and east by adjoining corps. It would not be a defence *in situ* but a flexible and delaying defence of manoeuvre—admittedly a dangerous form of defence by untrained forces, but the best available under the circumstances.

As regards County Wexford, the meeting of the brigades' commanders to finalise the plans was held in the house of Comdt Seamus Rafter. This meeting was attended by Staff Captain

Liam Mellowes. He represented GHQ and came to lay before the meeting the specific requirements of GHQ, to be carried out by the Wexford brigades, north and south. None of those present were told of any specific date for a rising, but all were cautioned of the very confidential nature of the discussions; nor was anything committed to writing for obvious reasons.

The first requirement of GHQ was that the Wexford Volunteers should keep open the line of communication between Dublin, Wexford, Waterford and Cork. Immediately the order was received from GHQ, all the Volunteers of County Wexford were to be mobilised at Enniscorthy, the centre of the county. Here there was to be a redistribution of arms, necessitated by the fact that while some corps were reasonably well armed, considering the circumstances, others were very poorly armed. A commissariat was to be set up for the provisioning of the men in the field. As soon as this task was done the local police barrack was to be invested. Every effort was to be made to achieve a quick surrender and the arms and ammunition taken at once and distributed to the corps. Meanwhile small detachments were to be sent at once to take the police barracks in outlying localities.

This achieved, the main body was to be split into two brigades, as strong and well armed as possible. One was to be despatched to New Ross and the other to Rosslare. Here they were to occupy defined positions.

At Rosslare the objective was to vigorously oppose the landing of British forces. They were not to attempt a fight to a finish, but to retire when no longer able to maintain their positions effectively and to continue to harass the enemy in his progress inland.

At New Ross the task was to watch the Waterford entry, to attack any force landed there from the flank and to harass their progress inland.

If for any unforeseen reasons these plans were incapable of being put into force the brigades were to fall back on Enniscorthy, re-form and, marching through Wicklow, threaten the rear of the Curragh from the south. It was expected that troops sent over from England would be mainly raw recruits and that, with our superior knowledge of the local terrain, we could outmanoeuvre them and even manage to attack them in the rear. The great obstacle to every plan was the pitifully small amount of arms and ammunition with which to carry out any assault. In the whole county there were not more than one hundred really effective rifles and the amount of ammunition available for them would not last beyond a few hours of stiff fighting. Hence it was repeatedly emphasised that anything like a prolonged fight was to be avoided at all cost, and manoeuvre and harassing tactics mainly resorted to.[30]

It was late at night before I was free to cycle home. Mellowes elected to see me 'past the gander'; actually we walked together to Scarawalsh where the hump-back bridge spans the river Slaney. This was practically half-way between Enniscorthy and the village of Ferns, and was the scene of many of our combined exercises. It was a beautiful night, calm and still, with a full moon riding high in the cloudless heavens. We were sitting chatting on the parapet of the bridge when the cathedral clock struck the witching hour of midnight. We decided to call it a day, shook hands and parted, he to travel to the west to take up his own command there, I to travel to Dublin. It was destined to be the last time we ever met. He was executed for his part in the civil war which followed the Anglo-Irish Treaty. Such is the way of revolution. But he was a gallant soul.[31]

After the Rising much unmerited criticism was directed against the plans for the seizure of Dublin city. In particular the failure to take Dublin Castle and to occupy the Telephone Exchange were emphasised. But those critics overlook the confusion and dispersion of city Volunteers due to the cancellation. Both these vital objectives were covered by the plan, but there were not enough men available for the implementation of the full plan.

The failure at Dublin Castle was due to the accidental firing of a shot which alarmed the sentries and police at the main gate and led to the slamming and locking of the great gates. Once this was done the castle was impregnable to the small force sent against it.

The only act open to justifiable criticism was the entrenchment in St Stephen's Green. This was certainly a blunder. It was a relic of the old barricades idea. It should never have been resorted to.[32]

Trinity College should, and probably would, have been occupied only for the scarcity of personnel at the eleventh hour. Its occupation would certainly have relieved my situation in O'Connell Street.

The one really big flaw in our effort was the decision to stand fast and fight in Dublin. But when one remembers that the 'blood sacrifice' group were firmly in control, this decision, even though wrong from a military point of view, is at least understandable. The decision to surrender unconditionally was severely criticised by very many of the participants themselves. But again the leaders were not blood-thirsty persons. No matter what the circumstances and conditions were, they had one specific purpose in view: in striking in Dublin and maintaining their positions there for a whole week they had achieved their purpose. They had no desire whatever for unnecessary loss of life and destruction.

On balance it is plain that, under the circumstances and conditions of the time, a rising was inevitable. The surprising thing about it was that Dublin Castle and the British military were caught so completely by surprise. On the whole the plans for the Rising were as technically sound as the circumstances and resources available permitted. Given a successful landing of adequate arms, free co-operation and simultaneous action all over the country, they would have gone far in the attainment of the ultimate objective.

That they could have resulted in a complete military victory for the Volunteers and Citizen Army is certainly open to conjecture. It was a political as well as a military necessity for the British to suppress the Rising quickly. I know personally that the British military authorities were gravely perturbed, once they had the Rising in the city under control, about the possibility of sporadic risings in the provinces. Had the Dublin forces broken off the engagement and retreated to the country, as they could have done, before the British cordons closed in, the British would have been faced with a very awkward situation. A running fight certainly would have followed for the country corps were just as anxious for a fight as the city ones.

As regards the positions held in the city and their defence, it may be said that the plan, and Connolly's instructions to the several commanders concerning it, amounted to a policy of static defence. This method is rarely effective and is particularly dangerous when the defenders are opposed by a force superior in equipment and numbers. And so it was in our case.

What the situation really called for was a holding of the seized positions by light or skeleton forces, and the pushing out of strong patrols along the obvious routes of the enemy's advance lines. It would be the task of such patrols to throw up as many obstacles as possible to the enemy's advance and, by engaging him well in advance of the occupied posts, force him to deploy prematurely; then to send round him small flanking parties in an effort to force a retirement. The main purpose of such tactics would not be to engage the enemy heavily, but to halt and delay his advance as far from the occupied posts as possible, thus gaining valuable time as well as inflicting casualties.

It is highly probable that the holding of the city by the Volunteers in this manner could have been prolonged into the second week at least. An active and enterprising defence sets many problems to an attacker.

But Connolly's instructions, as general officer commanding Dublin, tied the post commanders rigidly to the defence of the positions they first occupied. This enabled the British forces, once they really got on the move, to advance rapidly to the several positions held by the Volunteers, Citizen Army and Hibernian Rifles. Once they got there and brought artillery into action the end was already in sight. Even if there had been no countermanding order and the full strength of the Volunteers, Citizen Army and Hibernian Rifles had been available that fateful Monday morning, the result, insofar as the city was concerned, would have been the same.

The only alternative was disengagement and retirement to the country before the British ring was completed. But the rigidity of the static defence policy, based as it was on Connolly's sincerely held belief that artillery would not be used against us, had blocked any serious consideration of such an alternative. Hence, defence for more than a week was not possible.

All this is no reflection on the military genius of James Connolly. His preconceived and mistaken notion of what 'capitalism' *per se* was capable of caused a blind spot in his mentality. This prevented him from realising that, once the crisis had arisen, the military would be in control. They would follow the best methods of militarily dealing with the crisis with the least possible loss to their own forces, and the hated 'capitalists' would not be in a position to interfere with military decisions. In any case they were Irish capitalists.

There are two pre-Rising controversial points which I must deal with before passing on to the actual fighting. The first is the alleged secret arrest or kidnapping of James Connolly and the other is the position of Arthur Griffith.[33]

No one who had even a superficial knowledge of the character of James Connolly would dream of arresting him in an effort either to restrain him from premature action, or to persuade him to a particular line of action. He was not merely an individualist, he was also a dedicated socialist. He might be overcome in an argument or overwhelmed by circumstances, but he would never be bullied.

It was at one time a proud boast of international socialists that they were capable of preventing any future wars. They had declared their ability to do so by a universal 'down tools' strike on the eve of any threatened war. On the face of it, the prevention of war by a unified and solid international labour organisation ordering a universal 'down tools' was not so very far-fetched. Whether Connolly believed wholeheartedly in all this high-sounding bombast it is now quite impossible to say. But it is surely reasonable to conclude that he did believe in the honesty and solidarity of world socialists. He was far too sterling a character to continue being one if he did not.

His first disillusionment came with the 1913 Dublin strike. He was by no means as adequately supported in that dispute as he had a right to expect from his world comrades. Then the utter collapse of all this tall talk on the outbreak of the First World War must have been a devastating shock to a man of Connolly's temperament.

So he sought out the solitude of the countryside and walked and walked whilst he fought out the issue with his own conscience. Is it any wonder that on his return he should exclaim 'I've been through hell!' In such a predicament it was not in his great heart to indulge in futile denunciations and denials. He had fought the matter out in the bitterness of his own heart, and there was no more to be said.[34]

It is significant, too, that he should send Cathal O'Shannon, a veteran Belfast nationalist and trade unionist, to the IRB with the intimation that he was prepared to take the oath. He no longer held to a personal dream of a 'workers' republic' but placed himself and his followers under the discipline and leadership of the Brotherhood.

In hardship, hunger and toil he had faithfully followed a particular road only at journey's end to find it led to a futile illusion. He no longer looked towards and laboured for a single class, but gave his life to the whole nation. 'When we strike,' he had said, 'we will be no longer Irish Volunteers and Citizen Army, but only the Irish Republican Army.'

Arthur Griffith, too, had his dreams. But he was no idealistic dreamer. He was, above every other quality, a far-seeing and practical man. I would go so far as to say quite definitely that he was the only leader of my generation who possessed the attributes of sound statesmanship. His defects of character, if they could be called such, were a complete lack of personal ambition in the service of his country and an abiding loyalty to those set over him. If others had possessed the same degree of personal loyalty and less personal ambition the subsequent history of our country would have been quite a different story.

Arthur Griffith was a long-standing member of the IRB. He was by no means an opponent of an Irish Republic. Looking abroad, he could see no prospect of its immediate realisation but that did not turn him from his allegiance to the IRB.

When, in November 1913, the Irish Volunteers were formed, he took his place in their ranks. By this act he did not forgo his national policy enshrined in 'Sinn Féin'. His powerful pen and mental clarity were given unsparingly to the support of both movements. Just as he had supported the Gaelic League and every other Irish-Ireland movement he now supported the Volunteers. The fullness of his great heart embraced all who truly loved Ireland.

Arthur Griffith did not take part in the Easter Rising for the very good and sufficient reason that he had received a direct personal order from the military council not to do so. He was deliberately reserved in this special manner in order that he might be able to carry on his great work for the nation in the event of the failure of the Rising.[35]

How nobly and unselfishly Arthur Griffith carried that work to a successful conclusion is quite another story.

Chapter 3
Easter

It was surely a reasonable assumption that the capture of the *Aud* arms ship and Sir Roger Casement together with the drowning of the three technicians off the coast of Kerry would have alerted Dublin Castle and the British military command to the fact that really serious events were afoot. In the words of Pearse it had now become a race between us and Dublin Castle in real earnest.[36]

At a meeting of the military council Eoin MacNeill was removed from his post as chief of staff of the Volunteers and his place taken by Comdt General Joseph Mary Plunkett.[37] This was not as unilateral a change as might appear on the surface. It was certain that, on the eve of hostilities, the position would have to pass to someone else as it was a post for which MacNeill was temperamentally unfitted as well as lacking in all military experience.

The immediate problem, from late on Saturday night to the following Monday morning, was to hold a sufficiency of Volunteers standing by quietly and unobtrusively. On the publication of the order of the day very many, in good faith, had gone off to spend the Eastertide in their own individual fashion. It was not a problem of much concern to Connolly as he could much more easily keep the members of the Citizen Army standing to. The position had, through unforeseen circumstances, so evolved that it was no longer possible to avoid an immediate rising if we were not to allow the British to get in the first strike. However, the order of the day did so seriously affect the effective strength of the Volunteers immediately available as to render it virtually impossible to carry out in full detail all the plans for the seizure of the city.

To a certain extent the order of the day had affected myself. One of the couriers sent to the country with the order was my friend J. J. O'Connell. I had been unable to contact him personally since my arrival in the city and consequently, at this critical hour, moves which were taking place behind the scenes were entirely unknown to me. I was in the unhappy position of a mariner at sea without a compass.

But the one outstanding thing about the whole confused situation was the complete absence of any precautionary measures by the British authorities. The very least one might expect was the holding in barracks of an adequate, quick-striking force to deal with any untoward event. But no such precaution was taken: it is impossible to decide whether this was due to overconfidence or stupidity. And it may also be taken that much of the evidence tendered at the royal commission of enquiry into the cause of the Rising was coloured by the lesson of events and the necessity of making out a good case for the authorities in Dublin Castle.

———

Liberty Hall, which I saw for the first time that Easter Sunday morning, was a substantial building battlemented, if I may properly use the term, by a big metal railway bridge which stretched between it, the Custom House and the harbour. Across its front was a long scroll of white cloth bearing in large capital letters the statement: 'WE SERVE NEITHER KING NOR KAISER'. In view of all the circumstances of the moment this could only be regarded as a forthright and defiant declaration of war. Legally and technically, at least, we were all supposed to be the king's subjects and His Britannic Majesty was at war with the kaiser! It was typical of the determination and belligerency of James Connolly, just as it was symptomatic of the state of confusion and indecision of the official mind, that it had been allowed to flaunt brazenly there for weeks.[38]

It was a critical seesaw position for our opponents. For valid reasons arising out of the bad war situation the British did not want an explosion in Ireland; on the other hand Dublin Castle wanted to get out and 'squelch the Irish'. At this critical period England had, fortunately for us, the wrong prime minister. H. H. Asquith was by nature a Tory and not a Liberal. His chief secretary, Augustine Birrell, was a man of letters rather than a man of political decisiveness and prompt action. So far as the natural wishes of the permanent officials in Dublin Castle were concerned, Birrell was their old man of the sea. Hence Connolly could publicly flaunt his defiance with impunity.[39]

A number of working men, dressed in their Sunday best, were standing around the railings chatting and smoking in groups. There was an air of peace and tranquillity about the place. As I went up the steps I glimpsed, through the narrow side windows of the doorway, armed sentries.

My knock was answered promptly by a middle aged man wearing a bandolier and holding a rifle in his right hand.

Answering my question whether General MacDonagh was in the building, he said he did not know but would see. He then invited me inside but I replied that I would wait outside in the sun. Shortly he returned with a negative answer. He again invited me to wait inside but I declined with thanks. I stood on the top of the steps impatiently tapping my shoe with my walking stick. Actually it was the only weapon I had then on my person.

A few minutes later MacDonagh came round the corner from the quays. What a friendly, gentle and lovable little man he was! As usual he came with a song in his heart and a smile on his lips. He was dressed in a light coloured suit and appeared particularly debonair and gay. It was, indeed, difficult to picture him in the role of a fierce revolutionary.

As we shook hands he apologised for being late. We then entered Liberty Hall together, receiving salutes from the sentries. MacDonagh excused himself to me whilst he spoke to an officer, apparently the officer of the guard. Having said a few words to this officer, he turned to me, said he had to see one or two others, and suggested I find a seat. As it was such a glorious morning I replied that I would wait outside in the sun. It had been about 10 a.m. when MacDonagh arrived and it must have been just after noon when he finally emerged. He said that we would carry out an inspection of some of the battalion posts in the city.

We took an open-top tram to what was then Great Brunswick Street where a battalion headquarters of the Irish Volunteers was established. Here we found everything in apple pie order: sentries posted, passwords in operation. We passed upstairs to a room where the commander of the battalion had his office.

Sitting behind a desk was a sallow-complexioned man, wearing glasses and dressed in full officer's Volunteer uniform. He was introduced to me as Captain de Valera.[40] It was the first time I met the man who was destined to wield a profound influence on Irish national life in the years to come.

As he rose and formally saluted I thought him dour and aloof, even unfriendly. I did not, of course, expect him to fall on my breast and kiss me, continental fashion, but the impression left on me was of a character unIrish and foreign.

We only stayed a few moments. The 'inspection' was nothing more than a chat with de Valera on routine matters. Even so I was surprised to hear the commander say to MacDonagh that he would not act on any order he received unless it was signed, countersigned, timed and dated. I looked at him in surprise. I knew he was a college teacher but nothing more about him. What he had said, to be sure, was strictly in accordance with the book but I should certainly have expected a man of his position to have realised that in the adventure to which we were putting our apprenticed hands, and risking our lives, many an order would have to be acted upon that was not signed, countersigned, dated, much less timed.

When we were back again on an open-top tram I remarked to MacDonagh:

'We are going to have trouble with that officer.'

To which he replied with a smile:

'Oh, he's all right. A bit of a stickler for the book of rules. But he is all right.'[41]

It passed at that. Little either of us thought that we were speaking lightly of one of Destiny's spoiled children!

We did not call at any other post or headquarters but

journeyed about the centre of the city on top of trams for an hour or two. In the course of these peregrinations MacDonagh made a statement that surprised me. He said that Count Plunkett, who had returned from a visit to the Vatican, had brought back a papal blessing on our efforts. For the moment I did not know what to say. Naturally the news pleased me very much but it seemed unusual. This claim has since been much discussed and very definitely denied by people not in a position to know whether it was true or not. One thing is certain: that Easter Sunday morning Thomas MacDonagh believed it implicitly and was very pleased with it. What Irish Catholic would not be pleased with it? Nor did he say it to keep my own courage up, since there was no need for such a prop.

The only person I know who has consistently defended this claim—apart from Count Plunkett—is the veteran patriot, Brian O'Higgins, who in one of his publications made the following truly remarkable defence of the claim of the receipt of the papal blessing on Easter week:

Round about 1932 open expression was given to this belief [denial of the blessing] and men and women known as ardent Republicans took part in the debunking of a preposterous story . . . A lady well-known in Gaelic League circles wrote in a daily paper that those who accepted the story as truth offered insult to the Pope. How could he, the Vicar of Christ, bless bloodshed and strife. And several others joined in the wordy battle of annihilation, showing that the slave mentality was still rampant in our midst. They forgot, or never learned, that God Himself had sent His messengers direct to a simple, uneducated country maid in

France bidding her to go forth and gather soldiers about her to challenge the arrogant, unjust claims of her country's English invaders, to demand their withdrawal, and if they refused to leave and return to their own country, God told Joan of Arc to make war upon them until by force of arms she had redeemed France from the slavery of long years. Our scoffers, too, forgot that more than one occupant of the Chair of Peter had sent not only blessings but money and arms to Irish Patriots fighting the very same fight as the soldiers of 1916; and their forgetfulness led them to believe that the Pope would not even send a word of blessing to brave men, Catholic men, about to strike a blow against an invader for the freedom of their native land.

That was certainly a vigorous and unanswerable defence. So far as I know, no attempt has ever been made to meet it.[42]

In order to complete the record concerning this issue, I reproduce Count Plunkett's letter in the press:

I have heard that it is denied that I went to Rome immediately before the Rising of 1916 to communicate with His Holiness, Pope Benedict xv. I had no desire to publish information that at the time was not intended for the Press; but now I must disclose certain facts in the interest of truth.

About three weeks before the Rising I was, through my son Joseph, commissioned by the Executive of the Irish Volunteers (the Provisional Government) to act as their envoy on the Continent. One task given me I need not particularise here.

When it was carried out I went on to Rome, according to my instructions. There I was received in private audience by

His Holiness [and] for nigh on two hours we discussed freely the question of the coming struggle for Irish independence.

The Pope was much moved when I disclosed the fact that the date for the Rising was fixed, and the reason for that decision. Finally I stated that the Volunteer Executive pledged the Republic to fidelity to the Holy See and the interests of religion. Then the Pope conferred His Apostolic Benediction on the men who were facing death for Ireland's liberty.

Mr. John MacNeill will remember that he signed the Commission given to this (unnamed) Republican envoy to Rome. Some members of the Irish College in Rome will not have forgotten my visit there in 1916. On my return to Rome, in 1920, the same Pope congratulated me on representing the Republican Cabinet (when the Republic was functioning), as well as the martyr's family, on the occasion of the Beatification of Oliver Plunkett.

Back in Dublin on Good Friday, 1916, I sent in my report of the results of my mission, to the Provisional Government. In the General Post Office, when the fight began, I saw the portion of that paper relating to my audience with his Holiness in 1916.

(SIGNED) G. N. COUNT PLUNKETT.[43]

As we made no attempt to visit any other post or headquarters it was plain to me that MacDonagh was much more interested in noting if there were any signs of unusual activity on the part of the British authorities. We had learned that it was possible to gauge if there was any specific move afoot by the unusual coming and going of police, especially members of the detective

force. There are few better ways of carrying out such obser-
vations than from the top of an open tram.

Life seemed very normal in the city. So MacDonagh decided
to call it a day. Instructing me to report at Liberty Hall at the
same time the following morning we parted with mutual
expressions of good will.

————

Easter Monday morning was a glorious spring day, such as
seldom comes to our island. A warm, bright sun shone from a
cloudless sky over a gay city scene. The streets were crowded to
capacity. Thousands of people seemed to have come up for
Fairyhouse Races and most of them, like a great number of
citizens, were promenading the streets, obviously enjoying the
glorious weather, and savouring city life at its happiest and
most peaceful moment.

Children swarmed everywhere, racing and screaming at their
unrestrained play. Occasional Volunteers, in uniform, passing
here and there, were greeted with cheery curiosity. British
soldiers were to be met in every street, swagger canes under
arms, ogling the passing girls.

Indeed, it is no exaggeration to say that laughter and sunshine
were the keynotes of life in Dublin city on that fateful morning.
I had been out early and tramped the principal promenade
streets in every direction. In every quarter I found the same
light-hearted scene. Not a single sign of official perturbation.

Prompt to time, I was once more outside Liberty Hall. The
scene here was a repetition of that of the previous morning. My

enquiry elicited the information that General MacDonagh had not yet arrived. I was experiencing a bad feeling of restlessness and frustration.

MacDonagh had informed me that General Plunkett was ill, which did not greatly surprise me as we all knew he had been in poor health for some time. But I could not help wondering where I was to fit into the scheme of things. It was essential that I should get early information of what the exact position was if I were to put any degree of efficiency into my own particular job. More and more I came to regret having delayed, even for good local reasons, reporting to GHQ.

However, General MacDonagh arrived just after me. He was told at the door that 'all the others are upstairs'. We stood for a moment on the top step chatting on aspects of things in the city. He then instructed me to report at once to General Plunkett, chief of staff, to whom I had been appointed. He told me that Plunkett was then in a private nursing home in the north side of the city. It was in fact Miss Keogh's Nursing Home in Mountjoy Square. He told me he had just come from seeing Plunkett.

I had to enquire from him how I would get to the home. As we parted with a handshake and a 'good luck' wish, he smilingly remarked that we would probably not see each other for some time. It was in fact the last time I was ever to see this great-hearted patriot. He was shot to death, after a drumhead court martial, by the British, because he loved his country better than his life.

When I was shown into the private ward of the nursing home I was shocked at the appearance of my chief. If ever death had laid its mark openly on a man, it was here. He was sitting on the side of the bed. A nurse was bandaging his throat, and a tall pale-faced young man was hovering about somewhat restlessly.

The chief shook hands and introduced the young man as Michael Collins, his aide-de-camp. It was easy to see why this young man was chosen as Plunkett's ADC—his obvious vigour and youthful energy were assets to a man already weakened not only by great mental strain but also by grievous ill-health.

I can't say that, at the time, I was much impressed with Collins. He appeared to be silent to the point of surliness, and he gave my hand a bone-creaking squeeze without saying a single word. Little I guessed how intimate we were to become in subsequent years.[44]

Another nurse came in just then, apparently the matron. Both nurses sought to persuade Plunkett to go back to bed, but with a gentle smile and a wave of his hand he put their exhortations aside. The bandaging finished, Collins helped him into his tunic, after which Plunkett told him to call a cab. When the cab arrived he had to be assisted down the stairs. Tears were in the nurses' eyes as they followed us to the door. When settled in the cab, one of us on each side of him, he gave the word to drive to the Metropole Hotel where he had a suite of rooms. As we jogged along the streets the chief lay back against the rear cushion of the cab, his eyes closed most of the time.

The hotel vestibule was crowded with British officers, even the doorway had its quota of gay lieutenants. Our companion lay for a second or two looking out, then turning to Collins he said:

'You lead the way straight to my apartment. I will follow close behind, then the Commandant. I will be all right. Tell the cabbie to wait.'

As Collins got out he barked up at the driver the one word 'wait' and turned to assist our chief to alight. As soon as the uniformed figure with the heavily bandaged throat appeared all talk and laughter ceased amongst those at the door. The vestibule was full of talk and laughter, but as we entered complete silence fell, and curious glances were given us as we moved slowly in. Room was readily made for us to pass on, but the silence was maintained until we entered the upper apartment. Here the chief stretched out on the bed and rested after climbing the stairs. Then he struggled to a sitting position on the side of the bed. He told Collins to open a large cabin trunk which was on the opposite side of the room, and remarked as Collins did so: 'They haven't been searching my things.'

Reposing on the top of the contents I saw the large manuscript of my textbook on training for the Volunteers. A supply of maps and three automatic pistols—which I was surprised to see—were extracted. He handed one to each of us and also gave me an Ingersol pocket watch. He then had his Sam Brown put on after which he said:

'You lead out and down the stairs. I and the Commandant will follow. We must not allow ourselves to be arrested under any circumstance. If necessary we must shoot our way out but not unless it's necessary. There is an intelligence officer in the vestibule, a stout dark man. If he attempts to interfere he is to be shot at once.'

As soon as we emerged the babble of talk ceased and everyone present turned and watched in silence our progress downstairs. Sure enough the stout, dark officer stood right at the bottom of the stairs with one hand on the newel post, a quiet smile on his features. It is strange what trifling details stand out sometimes in tense situations. Our chief used the banister to assist him down. I still had my light raincoat with me and my walking stick and had the pistol, safety catch off, under the coat.

As we made the bottom step the intelligence officer bade us a friendly 'good day' to which the chief and myself replied in similar fashion. Otherwise he made no move of any sort. I have often wondered what would have been the result if any of them had been tipsy and made some well-intentioned but mistaken move. But they were all in a cheery mood and several followed the example of the intelligence officer as we crossed to the door. In the cab once more we three gave an audible sigh of relief, and Plunkett remarked, 'So far so good.'

We jogged along from the Metropole to Liberty Hall where the general headquarters staff were assembled. On the way the chief asked me if, in the event of our evacuating the city, Wexford would be a good county to fall back on. I answered at once, 'No', that for insurgents Wexford was a *cul de sac.*

The scene at Liberty Hall was one of considerable bustle and animation far different from the drowsy calm of earlier morning. Quite a number of armed and accoutred Citizen Army men were about the doorway and the footpath. No evidence of excitement was apparent on any face.

As the chief climbed out of the cab there was a general saluting. He stood smiling for a second or two, then returning the salutes he, helped by Collins, climbed the steps to the door which was instantly opened. Inside the place was jammed with armed Citizen Army men and all sorts of impedimenta. We began a slow climb up the stairs to a sort of attic room at the very top of the building.

Here in a small apartment were General Patrick Pearse and

General James Connolly and one or two others. They had a great welcome for Plunkett and hastened to get him a seat. I remained on the landing just outside the door. Pearse came out, shook hands and brought me into the room. On a small table, beside where I stood, was a little pile of what looked like posters. I turned sideways to read the top one. It was the historic proclamation of the establishment of the Irish Republic.

The sight of the Proclamation of the Republic on that table in Liberty Hall gave me a profound shock. I thought of all the speeches I had made in public, of all the articles I had written, in which I had specifically laid it down that the Volunteer movement would succeed above all other efforts solely because there was no secret organisation behind it.

For the very first time I now learned of the existence of the Irish Republican Brotherhood and that it was this secret organisation, more than any other factor, which had brought this glorious hour to fruition. I made no comment to anyone nor did anyone to me. But I had plenty of food for thought. Not that I was chagrined or felt let down by my comrades. I just felt small and insignificant. It is not a pleasant feeling especially when one is young and full of a healthy egoism.[45]

I subsequently learned that the Proclamation was printed in Liberty Hall as late as Easter Sunday night by three Dublin printers employed on the *Workers' Republic*. Type was scarce—a capital 'F' had to be turned into a capital 'E' with the aid of sealing wax, and a spare font of type had to be borrowed from an English printer named West in Capel Street. Yet by midnight, 2,500 copies of the most historic document in contemporary Irish history were run off. The printers were: Christopher J. Brady, Printing Department, Bank of Ireland; Michael J. Molloy,

Independent Newspapers; and William F. O'Brien, O'Reilly's Printing Works. Both Pearse and Connolly had co-operated in drafting the original copy.[46]

Meanwhile tremendous activity and bustle had been going on all over Liberty Hall. Messages were being continually brought up to Connolly. At last a young officer of the Citizen Army came up with word that all was ready. The copies of the Proclamation were rolled up and passed out to him.

To the earnest enquiries of his brother officers the chief of staff smilingly replied that he was 'all right'. All the passages had been cleared of gear and personnel, and only a few aged men stood about. As we passed they wished the 'Blessing of God' upon us. Slowly we went down the rather narrow stairs and out on to the street. The chief of staff made it unassisted. I never have witnessed a more perfect example of the power of will over the frail body.

The street was a sight. A fair contingent of the Citizen Army was drawn up in two ranks and under arms. There were a couple of horse-drawn lorries laden with a weird assortment of weapons, boxes and labourers' implements, such as pick axes, crowbars, sledges, etc. and also a couple of large, brand-new wickerwork hampers such as laundries use. In addition to their equipment the men in the ranks had extra guns and implements to carry.

Just then a motor car came round the quay corner and stopped with a clatter. A great cheer went up as The O'Rahilly was recognised. He had been amongst those who favoured a postponement until more arms were procured, but learning at the last moment that his comrades were 'going out' he had donned his uniform and, like the true nobleman he was, hastened to join them. He got out of his car and came over to shake hands with his brother officers who were unfeignedly glad to see him. Some of the stuff that was still lying around was piled in his car and he got back behind the wheel.[47]

A lady came hurrying on the scene, mounted the steps and began to implore Pearse to 'come home'. He made no reply to her importunities but kept turning away from her slowly in a most distressed manner. Connolly ended the painful scene by barking out an order.[48] The command to 'Form fours' was given. We placed ourselves at the head of the little column. General Connolly, as befitted his position as general officer commanding Dublin, on the right; General Pearse, again as befitted his position as general officer commanding all the forces, in the centre; General Plunkett on Pearse's left and I, as the only general staff officer present, on Plunkett's left. As he took his place Plunkett unsheathed a sword cane and threw away the sheath or stick. Collins took post immediately behind Plunkett.

As the order 'By the left, quick march' was given, a rousing cheer rang out from the rather imposing crowd who had by then gathered in front of Liberty Hall. We moved off at a brisk pace, swung left into Lower Abbey Street, and headed up towards O'Connell Street. We had, for good or ill, set out on a great adventure.

Chapter 4
The Insurrection Begins

As we marched towards O'Connell Street we must have presented an extraordinary spectacle. Everyone, except the officers, was so heavily overladen with weapons and implements that a corporal's guard would not have had a difficult task routing us. Scarcely a dozen of us were in a position to offer effective resistance.

Possibly the sidewalks had their camouflaged pickets. It would have been like Connolly's thoroughness to have provided for just such a contingency, but if there were any such flank guards I, for one, knew nothing about them and my heart was continually in my mouth with uncertainty. To have been flattened at the very moment we had begun would have been just too ridiculous.

As we marched up to the junction with O'Connell Street pedestrian traffic paused to let us pass and we received several cheers. A quick glance up and down this broad thoroughfare assured us that no immediate danger threatened us. On our 'right incline' across the main city artery vehicular traffic also came to a good-humoured halt. Actually we did not cause any undue excitement as the many previous marches, mobilisations and mock manoeuvres had accustomed the bulk of the citizens to our presence on the streets.

Swinging up along the opposite side of O'Connell Street I observed that practically all the British officers in the Metropole Hotel had congregated on the footpath and were laughingly enjoying the sight of the 'comic opera' army. One could not blame them. To any professional soldier we must have presented a very funny sight. Without any untoward incident and to the accompaniment of a fair amount of friendly cheering we duly arrived in front of our objective.

As we came abreast the main entrance of the GPO, in the middle of O'Connell Street, the command rang out: 'Company halt. Left turn.' Knowing what was coming next Collins and I anticipated events a little by linking our arms in Plunkett's and moving off towards the doorway. Then Connolly's stentorian voice rang out: 'The GPO, charge!' It was well we had anticipated the movement even by seconds as otherwise Plunkett might have been swept off his feet as the party with one wild cheer made a determined rush for the doorway. The large public office was crowded with people and officials. Just as we got inside Connolly's voice again rang out in a very determined tone, 'Everyone outside.'[49]

For a moment there was a stunned silence. It seemed for that fraction of time as if the people and officials were under the impression that the peremptory order had reference only to the members of the Citizen Army. As soon as it was realised that it referred only to the public and officials present there was a panic rush for the exits. Several officials left their counters and bolted without waiting to secure either hats or coats. The moment the public offices were closed Connolly's voice again rang out: 'Smash the windows and barricade them!'

This order was carried out with great gusto. A female voice

outside rose piercingly above the din, 'Glory be to God, the divils are smashing all the lovely windows.'

There is no doubt that some sections, at least, of the Citizen Army which carried out this occupation had been specially selected for the job and had been made quite familiar with the intricacies of the vast building. Immediately we entered, a small detachment swept upstairs, took the British military guard by surprise, disarmed them and made them prisoners; others swept through to the yard where they seized the van entrance, admitted the horse lorries and The O'Rahilly's motor car and then locked the gates.

The party upstairs, having overcome the soldiers, began to clear out the staff. These came down in an irregular stream, some looking about them in frank curiosity, others in rather a dazed condition. In a short space of time the word came through that the building was free of everybody except ourselves.

It was just after noonday, 24 April 1916. In this way the GPO was quickly, quietly and even bloodlessly seized. The general staff headquarters of the Irish Republican Army and the seat of the provisional government of the Irish Republic was established.

When we got safely inside the main door General Plunkett shook himself free of Collins and myself and leaned against a counter smiling at the feverish activity going on around him. There was a young British officer just inside the main door writing at one of the telegram ledges. Collins seized and searched him. He had no arms on his person. Telling him he was to consider himself a prisoner of war, we turned to an elderly policeman from the Dublin Metropolitan Police, who was standing in an imposing attitude nearby. As we told him to consider himself a prisoner, he asked rather pathetically not to be shot as he had done no harm to anybody.[50]

Collins then crossed to where Plunkett was still leaning against the counter. Pearse, whose voice had never once been raised, was chatting to him in a low voice. Collins then took the chief of staff upstairs where, I was told later, he was put lying down.

I turned to assist in the work of barricading. It must sound incredible now, but the operation of seizing the GPO, in the very heart of the city, was carried out so quickly that few people in the great crowd which was promenading outside appeared to have any appreciation of what was actually taking place. The smashing of the windows alone seemed to bring home to them that they were in the midst of yet another Irish rising.

The work of efficiently barricading the big windows was no easy task to carry out. Every kind of material had to be hastily pressed into doing duty—books, ledgers, pads of money orders, telegram pads, files of correspondence, tables, loose desks. We had not long been at this work when a great cheer from the crowd outside informed us that the tricolour had been hoisted on the top of the building fronting the street. Just then the front door was opened and Pearse and Connolly, with a small escort, passed outside. Pearse read out the Proclamation and then had it posted up publicly.

The crowd kept its distance respectfully enough until the little party had passed back into the building when a rush was made to read the notice. Those in the rear called on those in front to read it aloud. Many sentences were loudly cheered and at the end there was a great ovation. This reading and posting of the Proclamation was an act formally setting up the Republic and provisional government.

All the members of the provisional government did not sit in the GPO as a cabinet, as is usually done. At least three— MacDonagh, MacDermott and Ceannt—were away commanding their posts.[51] If Pearse was the head and font of the younger school of Republicans, Tom Clarke was the Grand Old Man of the freedom movement. By that I do not mean in the sense of the passing of the years, as then he was by no means an old man, but in having given a whole lifetime of struggle, imprisonment and unparalleled loyalty to the cause of Irish freedom. Although Patrick Pearse and I were intimates, it is my view that writers and historians in subsequent years have, perhaps unconsciously, given Pearse a position of prominence in the movement which rightly belongs to Clarke. I trust the day is not far distant when some competent writer will do justice to the services and the memory of Tom Clarke. His quiet and somewhat shy unobtrusiveness would seem to have robbed even history of her due. In my frank and honest opinion, insofar as it was in the power of one man to bring an Irish insurrection into forthright activity, the credit for that achievement must go to Thomas J. Clarke.[52]

Almost from the very start of the occupation there were disconcerting false alarms. Suddenly the cry would go up outside: 'Here's the soldiers' or 'Here comes the military', and the crowd would begin to scatter. Immediately the work of barricading would cease, rifles would be grabbed and all hands would settle down in their positions to await an attack that never came. Amusing incidents were plentiful. Whilst I was superintending the barricading of a window in the centre of the main office, a tall individual wearing a peaked tweed cap and a stiff waxed moustache pushed a way for himself and his bicycle right up to the window. Looking up at me he asked in all seriousness:

'Are yeh guarding the place against the Shin Fayners?'

'Yes,' I replied, 'what about it?'

'I'd like to give a helping hand', came the reply.

My companion at the window was a rather beefy member of the Citizen Army. Hearing this reply, he grabbed his rifle, cocked it, and said quite savagely:

'Get to hell out of that or I'll blow yer bloody brains out.'

Soon contingents of women who were in receipt of the British army separation allowance—'Shawlees' they were popularly nicknamed at that time—arrived on the scene and the usual abuse began. The banter between them and members of the Citizen Army was frequently lurid beyond discreet repetition and left little to the imagination. It was idle telling the Citizen Army men to take no notice of these women. They believed in giving back as good as they got and, as some of the women seemed to be known personally to some of the men, the descriptions of personal character outraged all the precepts of Christian charity. That was bad enough, but when some other women took up the defence of the 'Shin Fayners' it looked as if a women's rebellion was going to break out any moment.

Whilst all this was taking place horse lorries had been sent out from the post office yard under escort to commandeer supplies of food and bedding. One of the first places so visited was the Metropole Hotel, which had by now been evacuated by British officers. In fact their evacuation of the hotel was as speedy as our seizure of the post office.[53]

Needless to say it was not long before a great concourse of people were massed in front of the GPO. Cheers and counter-cheers were going up from time to time. Incipient scuffles were taking place as the crowd began to take sides. It looked at one time as if a miniature civil war would break out. Then a large number of priests arrived on the scene. They appealed to the people to disperse quietly to their homes, but, at first, the appeals fell on deaf ears.

Curiosity was rampant. With some difficulty the clergymen formed a line across the street and began to try to push the people back in a direction north of Nelson Pillar. The crowd good-humouredly gave way before them, but as they pressed one lot backwards another crowd began to form up in the space they had cleared. Turning patiently, the clergy began to push the new crowd back towards O'Connell Bridge only to discover that as soon as they turned the old crowd began to follow after them to halt in front of the GPO. The priests spent some time trying to achieve the impossible. And whilst we laboured at the windows we had a grandstand view of the whole scene.

Meanwhile a tall British army officer came walking along smartly down the opposite side of O'Connell Street swinging a light cane. He looked continuously across at our side as he came along.

On Connolly's orders a couple of armed men went out and halted him. When they told him he was a prisoner he laughed, stepped in between them and came across the street with them into the GPO. It was plain enough that this was his real objective. After being searched he was taken upstairs and put along with the other prisoners. But his roving eye missed nothing during his passage through the main office.

Eventually a yell went up from the crowd outside that could not be mistaken in the reality of its overtones. The crowd scattered wildly in all directions, except for the foolhardy elements that always want to see the finish. Confirmation came down from the men posted on the roof that cavalry were approaching. Posts were instantly manned and orders were bawled out not to fire until the order was given.

In a short time a troop of what appeared to be mounted infantry came cantering down the street from the direction of the Parnell monument. Before they came fully abreast of the GPO, the order to fire rang out, a volley crashed forth and several saddles were emptied. The force beat a hasty retreat, leaving at least one dead horse behind. While falling off his horse one of the troopers lost his rifle, which did a short Catherine wheel in our direction. Instantly, a young newspaper boy, who had been crouching behind one of the front pillars, darted out, picked up the rifle, and began to rush towards us with it. Seeing this one of the Shawlees, who had been similarly concealed, ran forth with her arms outstretched in an endeavour to stop him. Quickly the youngster raised the rifle like a club, hit her a stiff clout with it, knocking her down, continued on his way and pushed the rifle through the window to us.

I cannot conceive anything more stupid than this sortie by mounted troops. They were probably only meant as an observation party, but for that purpose they were in the worst formation possible and their method of approach was casual in the extreme. Perhaps the British authorities thought we were squatting down in the centre of O'Connell Street waiting to be mopped up. Anyhow this repulse put great heart into all the men and a great deal of the tension of waiting was eased. Waiting is a nerve-wracking business even for regulars. It was afterwards claimed that this posse of troops were only out on routine exercise. Their casual attitude and their very hasty retreat would seem to bear this version out.[54]

The sortie gave rise to a ridiculous story that is still going the rounds to this day, namely, that Sinn Féiners tried to blow up Nelson Pillar. What actually happened is this. Part of our strange equipment were hand-made grenades. These, to a large extent, were small tin cans filled with metal pieces. They had a core of gelignite into which was sunk a percussion cap and a short length of fuse.

At the time of the sortie, one of the men on the roof tried to hurl one of these canisters at the mounted troops but, whether the fuse was too short or he held it too long, it exploded prematurely, inflicting what appeared to be serious injury on the thrower.

He was certainly a gory spectacle with a blood-covered face and suffering from shock. It was then decided to select a few of the canisters at random and test them. A party of armed men was sent out to clear away the crowd which had again gathered after the retreat of the troops, whilst those instructed in engineering carried out the test. The area of the pillar was selected as the safest place for such a test, and a couple of these home-made affairs were flung there, bursting with a tremendous bang. That was how this ridiculous story got around. Nothing was further from our thoughts that day than the statues and pillars of Dublin city.[55]

Eventually everything was shipshape or as much so as we could make it, though it was impossible to satisfy Connolly regarding the fortifications. He was continually inspecting them and wanting them strengthened. But no more could be done for lack of material. The time had come when I thought I could set about my own particular job. I went up to Pearse and told him I was now ready to begin the work of tabulating our positions in the city and marking the map. He consulted Connolly and the three of us made the rounds of all the offices on the ground floor.

In a corner office fronting the side of the Metropole Hotel Connolly said that in the event of a general assault I was to take charge there and at all cost to prevent the enemy from gaining a foothold there. Improvised methods of holding the door leading from this office to the main public one were put in hand on his orders.

Then Pearse sent a runner upstairs to the chief of staff for a large-scale map of the city. Procuring a small table and a chair, I now set about marking up our positions all over the city. This consisted first in marking on the map the regular military barracks in the city. I then took the bundle of command posts reports which Connolly handed me; some of these reports had come verbally to him at first and he had scribbled his own summary on a sheet of paper. They had been coming in all the time from the various occupation points directly to Connolly, who was personally cognisant of the entire situation. He and Pearse were the only ones, as far as I knew, who were. All these reports had to be sorted out and marked up on the map. Then a summary of reports had to be made. This summary and the marked maps enabled the two general officers in command to have a clear picture of the actual situation from hour to hour and day to day.

Briefly the reports presented this picture. The first battalion of the Volunteers under Comdt Edward Daly had occupied the Four Courts. The second battalion under Comdt General Thomas MacDonagh had occupied Jacob's biscuit factory. The third battalion under Comdt Eamon de Valera had occupied Boland's flour mills. The fourth battalion under Comdt Eamonn Ceannt had occupied the South Dublin Union. The Citizen Army was mainly responsible for the GPO. The early reports did not mention outposts which these commands later pushed out once they had established themselves. These too had to be marked up. A contingent of the Citizen Army under Countess Markievicz for some extraordinary reason had gone out of the College of Surgeons and established themselves in trenches in St Stephen's Green. This tiny pleasance in the heart of the city was surrounded on all sides by very high buildings which completely dominated it. To occupy such a position was sheer lunacy because it was, from a military point of view, utterly untenable.[56]

There were two sad blanks in the overall picture: the failure of the surprise attack on Dublin Castle, and the failure through lack of personnel to occupy the Telephone Exchange in Crown Alley. This communication centre continued to function normally until late in the fight.[57]

Each of these occupation posts had detachments of Cumann na mBan and Fianna Éireann who acted as despatch couriers, nurses and cooks. Subsequent reports covered the establishment of smaller outposts in connection with the occupation posts headquarters. So far, one could be satisfied with the way in which the general plan for the seizure of the capital had been carried out by all the commanders concerned having regard to the resources of men and material at the disposal of the Irish Volunteers and Citizen Army. In considering these operations it must be borne in mind that the full strength of the Volunteer organisation was not available at the critical hour. Due to MacNeill's countermanding order, many in the Irish Volunteers and Citizen Army had gone off in good faith for holidays.

It was, however, in the provinces that the ill results of MacNeill's cancellation order were most grievously felt. With three exceptions—the mobilisations at Enniscorthy, the action at Galway by Mellowes and the remarkable fight at Ashbourne— the entire Volunteer force in the country was immobilised. Speculating after the event is usually a waste of time. Still one cannot help thinking that had there been no cancellation order issued to the country corps, and had the plans for the country— including the safe landing of arms from the *Aud*—been carried through as smoothly as the occupation of the metropolis, the situation confronting England would have been grave indeed.

The number of reinforcements which the garrison of the GPO received during the afternoon and evening was decidedly small. Once I had got my reports in order and summarised, and my map marked up, my personal duties were light. I frequently broke the monotony of tedious waiting by strolling around the ground floor offices talking with the men at their posts on different aspects of attack and defence. I cautioned them to be sure not to fire too rapidly or too soon, but to try to be certain of their target before pressing the trigger. The need for con- serving ammunition was very real, though compared with the country corps Dublin was fairly well supplied.

During one of these casual tours I solved the mystery of the large, brand-new laundry hampers which had so intrigued me when I first saw them being loaded on the horse lorries at Liberty Hall. They had been placed just inside the main entrance door on the north end of the GPO with the lids open. They were full to the brim with new oak police batons, which I presumed had been specially made for the Citizen Army. The batons were complete with wrist strap to prevent loss in a mêlée. It was evident that apart from the questionable useful-ness of the batons in an armed conflict, the authorities of the Citizen Army were determined that the workers of Dublin would never again be wholly defenceless at the hands of the Dublin Metropolitan Police. They were another sidelight on the character of James Connolly.

On a very large table, partly hidden by a screen, a most weird-looking collection of weapons was laid out. An assortment of daggers, bayonets, hatchets, cleavers, pistols ancient and modern, butchers' knives, boxes of cartridges, etc., was presided over by a stout, bespectacled young man who later became one of the great figures of our native insurance world, Michael O'Reilly. In his biography of Michael Collins, Rex Taylor located Michael O'Reilly in the Imperial Hotel in O'Connell Street. This is wrong. O'Reilly, to my personal knowledge, was never in the North Earl Street/Sackville Place position.[58]

In the event of a hand-to-hand struggle nothing was being left to chance. A determined man with a hatchet at close quarters is no mean opponent. Yet the collection struck me then as being essentially pathetic, showing the extent to which the army of the Republic was forced to improvise for lack of funds to buy proper weapons. At close-in fighting a man armed with an automatic pistol is a much more formidable opponent than a man armed only with, say, a butcher's cleaver. But I suppose, in the last analysis, the real deciding factor is the man.

I have just used the term 'army of the Republic'. And correctly so. Connolly had previously stated that when we struck we would cease to be separately the Citizen Army and Irish Volunteers and would become jointly the Irish Republican Army. That is the origin of the title which was so proudly borne in subsequent years. It was entirely consonant with the Proclamation.

As I sat at my table, during odd idle moments, I could not help contrasting the differences in character of our two commanders: the Generalissimo Patrick Pearse, and the commander of Dublin, James Connolly.

Connolly was always sharp and decisive, sure of every order he issued, with a plan clearly marked out in his own mind. Frequently brusque in his contacts, he was forever on the prowl, overseeing everyone and everything, and never quite satisfied with anything. He would have made a wonderful managing director of a big industrial concern. He was forever urging a further strengthening of the defences although all that could possibly be done had been done. Often he would give a blow to a pile of stuff in a window and when it wobbled or fell, as sometimes happened, he would ask irritably, 'What use is that?' But there was nothing else available.

Pearse was a complete contrast. Moving slowly about, he never sought to interfere with anyone or anything. His mind was obviously up in the clouds and at times he conveyed an impression of futility, as if he would be utterly helpless in a sudden and unexpected emergency. At the same time his mere presence was a tonic to everyone. There was a mystic atmosphere about his personality which inspired confidence and an urge to achieve great things. He was not just respected by the little garrison, he was almost worshipped. I suppose the explanation lies in the fact that the mystic holds a strong appeal to the Celt. One had the feeling that had he been born in the middle ages he would have been one of the great saints of Holy Mother Church. I think it was from this innate spirituality that his influence sprang. As I watched him slowly pacing up and down the length of the front office wrapped in his thoughts and apparently unconscious of everyone and everything, the thought occurred to me that he was contemplating dying a martyr's death for Ireland—a personal sacrifice he would gladly make for the sake of Kathleen Ní Houlihan.[59]

Some time between three and four o'clock a fashionably dressed dapper little man, whom I knew very well, came into the GPO through the public entrance on the north end. He was Sean T. O'Kelly. Not only did I know him but practically everyone in the movement knew 'S. T.' as he was popularly referred to. Connolly happened to be down at that end talking to one of his own officers. With a casual nod and salutation to the commander of the whole Dublin area, O'Kelly came up to where Pearse was standing just at my table.

He nodded casually to myself and saluted Pearse in Gaelic. As I sat I looked at him with considerable amusement. We were, nearly all of us, dust covered and untidy. Not so our S. T. He was wearing a light grey suit, which fitted him to perfection, a straw hat, with multicoloured band and stylish tie, and carried a light walking cane. He presented a perfect picture of a young man about town.

He then gave a brief verbal report in my hearing which we already had in more detail from the various commanders. He completed his report with the very surprising statement: 'And now I will go home to my tea!' His *visit* had actually lasted less than ten minutes.

I have read and heard several accounts of S. T.'s part in the Rising, including his own. All these were to the effect that he had taken part in the occupation, and then had gone out with lorries commandeering food and bedding for the garrison. A neat little piece of fiction!

S. T. was one of the few at the mobilisation and occupation whom I would have known personally and he was never one to hide his light under a bushel. The commandeering was, in fact, carried out by a very small detachment of the Citizen Army. His first appearance in the GPO was between three and four o'clock, following which he 'went home for tea' and apparently stayed at home.

I could never find it in my heart to blame a man for funking a hopeless fight such as ours. We are not all cut from the cloth from which soldiers are made. But why set up to be a fire-eater after the fire has been quenched? He later became our ambassador in Paris, and an expensive one at that. In the debate on the Anglo-Irish Treaty he made a speech of which the peroration was: 'Let the fight go on and I will return to Paris!'

'By ____ you won't', fiercely retorted Collins, 'you will stay at home and fight with the rest of us.'

It is sufficient to say that S. T. ended his political career as president of the Republic of Ireland.[60]

And so the tedious day wore itself into the afternoon and late evening without any untoward events and the curious crowd waited outside for the feast of excitement that never came. A good deal of the high tension that prevailed at the start had eased and only expressed itself in a degree of restlessness and such muttered expressions as, 'Will they never come?' Such is the effect of waiting for strife to begin. The lack of prompt countermeasures against us was curious and there was much speculation as to the cause.

I had had nothing to eat since breakfast in the hotel, I was covered with grime from the work of trying to fortify the place, and I was physically beginning to feel the strain when at about ten o'clock I was relieved by, I think, Collins. I immediately started for the basement where I was told there were hot baths and food. Up to this I had not been anywhere in the great building except the ground floor offices.

I had only just reached the basement and was enquiring for the baths when a runner came and told me that I was wanted in the front office by General Pearse. Wondering if what we had been so patiently waiting for had come, I ran upstairs again. Everything, however, was just as I had left it. I went up to Pearse and saluted. He told me to report to Connolly. Looking around I saw General Connolly standing in front of ten armed men who were drawn up in front of the main entrance door. I ran up and saluted at once. Connolly said:

'A report has just come in that the British have occupied Amiens Street Station in force. We anticipate an assault on our headquarters at any moment. You will take these men, occupy North Earl Street, break in and fortify the block down as far as the Imperial Hotel. As there is no post between the enemy and our headquarters you will defend this position to the last man. As you are the only experienced officer we have, you have been transferred to my staff. You will carry out these orders implicitly.'

I shuddered inwardly at the responsibility so very suddenly thrust upon my shoulders. To occupy and fortify a whole block of city buildings with only ten men and in face of an imminent

assault! I took a quick look at the men. With the exception of
Gerald Crofts, whom I had met in Gaelic League circles and was
familiar with, they were all strangers to me and I to them. In
addition to rifles and bandoliers they were laden with crowbars,
sledges and so on. In the flurry of the moment I could not recall
exactly where North Earl Street lay and had to enquire. Crofts
spoke up at once saying it was only across the way and that they
all knew it. Then Connolly added, 'We will send you reinforcements as soon as we can'.

Pearse had come up by this time and both he and Connolly
shook hands with me. Saluting them both I gave the order. The
big doors swung open and we marched out of the GPO.[61]

Chapter 5
I Become a Post Commander

As soon as we emerged from the GPO, a half-hearted cheer went up from the crowd of the idle curious gathered outside, principally of the working class and the poorer elements of the city. They had been moving restlessly about. Apparently the long waiting with nothing of a really exciting nature happening had cooled their ardour irrespective of what side they took. Having got clear of the footpath I gave the order to double. The shuffling trot of the laden men quickened the interest of the onlookers, who seemed to think that at last something worth watching was about to take place and proceeded to keep pace with us.

A hasty look at both sides of the street corner convinced me to begin on the right-hand side, or Noblett's corner as it was then. The first task was to break into this establishment which would give us a fairly wide angle of fire. It was also the one directly opposite the GPO.[62]

The door of the ground floor corner premises was locked. In fact, all the floors of this particular building were abandoned, including the Pillar Cafe, which was on the first floor. The crash of a sledgehammer against the panel of the door brought a shocked gasp from the crowd at our heels—as if they had sustained a physical hurt.

As we entered and proceeded upstairs, the bolder elements of the crowd, avid with curiosity, started to follow. Turning back, I ejected them and placed an armed sentry on the door with orders to admit no one but known Volunteers or Citizen Army personnel.

When we reached the first floor the work of breaking out windows and barricading them had to start once more. It was also essential to get a barricade across the street as quickly as possible to form at least an obstruction to an advancing enemy. So when the windows of the lower side of the Pillar Cafe were fortified and loopholed underneath, I ordered the throwing out through the windows of the remaining furniture. As the first articles came flying out through the windows a cry of astonishment went up from the onlookers.

Then as a brocaded armchair fell out, one of the Shawlees, a big buxom young woman, yelled to a companion: 'They're throwing away the lovely furniture, Mary. Come on!' And straight away she seized the armchair and started to carry it off. If this kind of thing once got started it would certainly be farewell to my barricade. There is nothing more lawless and irresponsible than a crowd that has got out of hand.

So far the crowd in O'Connell Street had been very well behaved. They had been possessed of a mixture of mere curiosity and uncertainty, perhaps tinged with a little fear. Moreover, nothing had been thrown out of the GPO, because no barricades were erected around it. But as soon as our barricade material appeared, flung out and apparently useless, the natural cupidity of the human being flared. It was certain it would spread and that the crowd would not be content with seizing what was flung out but would enter the building and start wholesale looting. In fact, that was exactly what happened later on.

So I dashed down the short flight of stairs immediately, pulling my automatic pistol out of my pocket as I did so. Fortunately the armchair was big and heavy, and the woman had only gone a few paces down the street when I overtook her, pointed the pistol at her and ordered her to take the chair back and put it where she got it.

Being a bit tipsy she started an argument for which I had neither the time nor the inclination. Telling her to take it back instantly, I gave the chair a slight push. She looked at me rather belligerently and then, to my great relief, turned and carried it back putting it down with a bump. The danger lay in the fact that under such circumstances it would be so easy to rouse a crowd to unreasoning anger which would have rendered our situation extremely delicate.

The woman, however, saved the situation. She suddenly flung out her two arms, the sides of her shawl gripped in her two hands, and tried to embrace me, calling me her darling young officer. I quickly side-stepped, and so determined was her purpose that she staggered and nearly fell. This put the watching crowd in good humour and they cheered her lustily.

I seized this favourable moment to make a short address to the people. I said we had risen to free our country; that we were staking our lives in the effort and that we expected the help and goodwill of every true Irishman and woman. This got to the crowd who cheered my few words. Indeed, they seemed ready to cheer at the slightest provocation. The sentry at the door had moved over to my side, and the men at the windows held their guns at the ready. Signing to them to carry on I proceeded to

pace up and down, trying to arrange the stuff to the best advantage as it fell to the ground. Some of the younger men then
came to help me. Instructing them the way I wanted the
materials placed, I gave a sigh of relief and left them to their
self-imposed task. All danger from the crowd had passed, at
least temporarily.[63]

They must have observed our difficulty in the GPO because
six more armed men came across as a reinforcement. Putting
one to guard the slowly forming barricade, I selected another,
told him to go inside, give his arms and equipment into the care
of a comrade (he was a sharp-looking youth dressed in civvies)
and then go down and scout around Amiens Street railway
station.

I told him we needed to know whether there were any British
soldiers there and, if so, approximately what their numbers were
and if they were there for occupation of the railway or massing
for an attack on the GPO. He asked me how he was to know that.
I told him that if the number of troops was small and if they
were barricading the place as we had the GPO, then they were an
occupation force; if, on the other hand, there was a large number
of troops present, and no great effort was being made to fortify,
then they were an attacking force. He set off at once.

My next task was to superintend the punching of a large hole
in the party-wall between the Pillar Cafe and the next premises.
This was what the crowbars and sledges were for. First, however,
it was necessary to glance at the fortification of the windows.
Here a shock awaited me. Connolly's plans of occupation and
fortification were really excellent, but the men seemed to have
been very indifferently instructed in the details of the work. The
windows of the cafe fronting O'Connell Street were very large,

with wide metal ledges jutting outward, from the front edge of which ornamental metal railings rose up to a height of about eighteen inches. The men had broken out all the glass, upended tables and placed them, legs upward, on the ledge and on top of the metal railings. They had then partially filled the tables with table napkins, etc.

One middle-aged Citizen Army man was stretched out full-length on this improvised bed, his Mauser rifle thrust forward. From his knees up, his entire body projected beyond the front wall of the line of buildings. He was a sitting duck for a sniper. Relieving my harassed mind with a few lurid words I ordered the tables to be removed, the metal work to be smashed to avoid the danger of ricocheting bullets, and loopholes to be punched in the wall underneath the windows and on the level of the floor.

Then putting my head out of the window and seeing the window of the next premises (they were not always on the same level), I selected the place to punch the hole through the party-wall. Just then the sentry at the door yelled up that the officer was wanted. Going down I was surprised to see Paul Galligan standing just outside. Paul was a draper's assistant in Bolgers of Enniscorthy and a member of the Volunteers in that town. He was as surprised to see me as I was to see him.

Like hundreds of Volunteers, when he heard of the cancellation order he had come up for Fairyhouse Races. Then, learning late in the evening of the Rising, he had tried to get into the GPO. Being unknown there he had come across to North Earl Street to try his luck. He was anxious to get back to Enniscorthy but even more anxious to contact GHQ, and find out if there was any message he could bring with him.

Hastily scribbling out a note of identification addressed to

Pearse, I gave it to him. Paul was a sound man and I would have liked to keep him with me but his duty lay to his comrades in Wexford. We shook hands and parted. I never laid eyes on him again though he went on to become one of Dublin's leading drapers.

Mounting the stairs again, I had just reached the scene of our labours, when I heard the sentry yelling for me once more. Cursing with irritation I trotted back. A barman complete with dark apron and rolled sleeves stood in the doorway.

'The boss wants to see the officer in charge', was his greeting.

'What the hell does he want?', I snapped.

My nerves were beginning to fray. I had had nothing to eat since breakfast and the excitement and responsibility were getting me down. What small degree of courtesy was in my make-up was oozing out.

'I don't know sir', he replied, 'but he said it was very important for you. And he doesn't want anyone but the officer in charge.'

'Where the devil is he, and why doesn't he come himself?', I asked.

'He is in the hall and he really does want to see you', was the answer.

In our delicate situation, we could not afford to miss anything that might be to our advantage; yet it was possible that I was being enticed off the premises on a fool's errand or into a trap. Drawing my automatic and slipping the safety catch, I told the man to lead on.

The pub was only a short distance down the street and I think was called Fagan's.[64] In the hallway a small, aged but active man was standing. He almost embraced me, and, with tears in his eyes, gave God thanks that he had lived to see that day. He said he had important information to impart to me and insisted on my accompanying him to the roof of his house. It seemed an outrageous request under the circumstances, but curiosity was getting the better of me by now.

So we started the weary climb to the roof. I reckoned I might as well learn the geography of the rooftops from his house as from that of the corner one. He never ceased his patriotic chatter all the way up; it was clear that he was consumed with a mixture of delight and a desire to be a participant in the affairs of the moment.

Once on the roof he began pointing out all the advantage points and identified all the principal buildings in the near and far distance. Then he told me he was an old Fenian, and that they had gone over all this in his youth. It certainly was an instructive few minutes. To receive it from an elderly city publican was surely a unique experience. I often wished to meet him in after years but never got round to it.

The bar was full and he requested me to get the customers out as he was anxious to lock up. Telling him to do it himself, I prepared to leave as I could not afford to be away from my post any longer. But he pleaded that under the circumstances they would pay no attention to him. So passing into the bar I made a brief address to those present and asked them to leave quietly. The more tipsy were inclined to begin arguing but they were overborne by their companions and in a few minutes the bar was clear.

Handing me the keys of the entire premises with a rather dramatic gesture, the old Fenian told me that the house and all its contents were mine. Slipping the keys into my pocket and thanking him, I left hurriedly.

When I got back my scout was waiting for me. He reported that there were no soldiers at Amiens Street station. I nearly swooned with relief. To have been vigorously attacked at this time, less than half ready to meet it and with the streets full of people, a big percentage of them half tipsy, would have been the very devil. It was a tremendous weight off my mind.

Another few men had joined the garrison whilst I was in the pub. Where they came from I did not know or enquire: as they were armed they were very welcome. Gerald Crofts reported that some Cumann na mBan ladies had also joined the garrison and were at the back in one of the kitchens.

'For God's sake, Gerald,' I said to him, 'get them to make me a cup of tea or I'll just crumple up like an empty sack.'

Like the good fellow he was, he ran off at once and in a matter of minutes I was called down to the kitchen, where a really sumptuous tea was spread out for me. It tasted like the nectar of the gods and put new life into me. There were four Cumann na mBan ladies in the detachment, armed with bandages, surgical appliances, etc. I regret I am unable to recall any of their names after this lapse of time and indeed I only met one of them after, at the official reopening of the GPO. There never were more brave or more devoted women in the history of mankind.[65]

As I supped, I asked the senior lady to make the rounds to find out if any other members of the garrison were in need of food and if there were, to arrange for their feeding at once. The original ten men who had come across from the GPO must have been in need of food by this time. Sending for Crofts again, I told him to start gathering in adequate supplies and to make sure that every available utensil was filled with fresh water.

W.J. Brennan-Whitmore in the uniform of the Irish Volunteers. This photograph was taken in January 1914, just two months after the formation of the Volunteers. He was officer commanding, Ferns Company in his native Co. Wexford.

At school: the earliest known photograph of W.J. Brennan-Whitmore. He is sixth from the right in the first full row, dressed in a sailor suit.

The junction of North Earl Street and O'Connell Street in the aftermath of the Rising. This photograph shows the position held by Brennan-Whitmore and his men. Part of the barricade which they threw across the top of North Earl Street can be seen in the foreground.

NORTH EARL ST FROM NELSON PILLAR, DUBLIN.

The ruins of the Dublin Bread Company building in Lower O'Connell Street. (© RTÉ Stills Library)

Another view of the junction of North Earl Street and O'Connell Street, seen from the top of Henry Street. (© RTÉ Stills Library)

The burnt-out shell of The O'Rahilly's De Dion Bouton in Prince's Street after the Rising. It was later buried under Hill 16 in Croke Park, which was built with rubble salvaged in the aftermath of Easter week. (© Corbis)

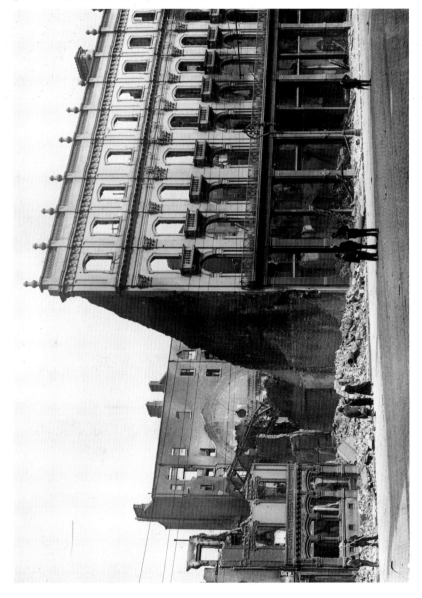

The ruins of the Imperial Hotel and Clery's department store, both close to Brennan-Whitmore's position during the Rising. (© Getty Images)

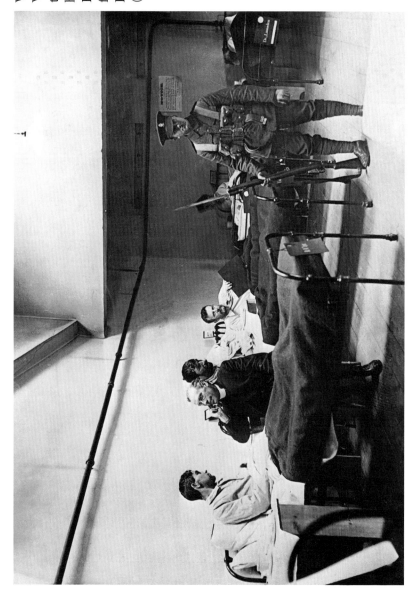

Wounded Volunteers in a temporary hospital in Dublin Castle following the Rising. (© Corbis)

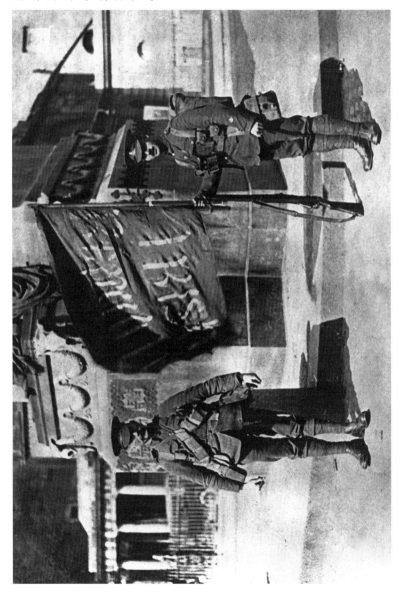

British soldiers stand at the Parnell Monument after the Rising, guarding the republican flag that had flown over the GPO. (© Corbis)

On Easter Monday, the first action involving the GPO garrison arose from a cavalry charge down Sackville Street by a troop of Lancers from Marlborough Barracks. Fired on from the GPO, three men died instantly and a fourth was fatally wounded. Brennan-Whitmore's comment was: 'I cannot conceive anything more stupid than this sortie by mounted troops.' The bodies of the fallen horses remained in the street all week. This photograph was taken on the Saturday, following the surrender. (© Corbis)

The intelligence staff, Army GHQ, 1926. Brennan-Whitmore is second from the right, seated.

Intelligence Staff, G.H.Q, 1926

James Connolly
(© Corbis)

Patrick Pearse
(© Getty Images)

Commandant Brennan-Whitmore in Free State Army uniform in the 1920s. He is photographed here with Fr John Mullan, whom he had first met while serving with the British Army Medical Corps in India before the First World War. It was Fr Mullan, then serving as a missionary in India, who first aroused his interest in Irish nationalism.

Conoentration Camp, Srongooh, Bala.

Frongoch camp in north Wales, where Brennan-Whitmore and his Volunteer colleagues were interned following the Rising. He later wrote a memoir, *With the Irish in Frongoch*, about his time there. (Courtesy of www.militaria-archive.com)

The author and his wife, photographed in the late 1940s.

The author and his wife on their wedding day.

The author in jaunty mood in O'Connell Street in the 1960s.

The author
in 1962.

One of the last
photographs of
the author, taken
in 1975 at a family
reunion. He died
two years later.

There was a danger that the water supply might be cut off at any moment and thereby render our situation very serious, especially if any of the garrison got wounded. I have often wondered why the British did not attempt to embarrass us in this way.

Checking on the workers of the garrison, I turned to my next most unpleasant task: persuading the people in residence in the immediate area to seek sanctuary elsewhere. They all demurred at first saying, naturally enough, that they had no other place to go to—at least not at such short notice and at so late an hour. But on it being explained to them that we expected to be attacked at any moment by British forces, in which event the area would become a shambles and their lives endangered, most of them agreed to go.

In only one place—a small draper's shop—was there real difficulty. It was owned by an aged, somewhat feeble man, wearing a long grey beard. He was furious with us and positively refused to leave. He had two daughters who told me that they had friends they could go to, but that their father had refused to listen to their pleadings. I urged his daughters to again put pressure on him and to tell him that it was necessary for all their safety to leave whilst there was yet time to do so. At last they succeeded in getting him to consent.

I tried to assist him down the stairs but my offer seemed to make him more furious still. When he reached the street and was slowly moving off towards O'Connell Street he called maledictions down upon us. Nor could I blame him. Only himself and the good God knew what personal sacrifices he had made in his lifetime to build up his business for his two girls; and now a crowd of 'young irresponsibles' were destroying his life's work and perhaps bringing them all to penury. It is a bad thing to be an imaginative revolutionary.[66]

Another bugbear that night was the number of men who wanted to join the garrison. The sentry at the door was continually calling me, from across the street or from upstairs, to attend to men who insisted on seeing the officer in charge. I could have quadrupled my little garrison in a short time if I had taken in all those who were volunteering their services. Something like the following conversation took place in each case.

'Yes. What do you want?'

'Please, sir, I want to join up and help.'

'Very good. Are you a member of the Citizen Army or the Volunteers?'

'No, sir.'

'Sorry. In that case I am unable to accept your services.'

'God's truth, sir, I do want to help. It would be an honour to be allowed to do so.'

'I want men badly, very badly. But what use would you be to me? You would only embarrass me. Since you are such a good Irishman, why did you not join the Volunteers or Citizen Army?'

'I never thought it would come to this, sir.'

Many of them had tears in their eyes as they turned away. I was, so to speak, hungry for men and help. But of what use would they have been? They did not know how to load, sight and fire a rifle, and even if they did I had no rifles to give them. They could have been of immense benefit at such work as labouring at the holes in the walls. I could have found a dozen tasks for them. But if a serious attack developed suddenly, how could I have got rid of them with safety to themselves? And in such an event how many of them would panic with disastrous effects on the rest of the garrison, all of whom had still to be tested under actual fire? It would have been the height of folly to take in a number of men whose antecedents were totally unknown to me and whose protestations of patriotism might well hide ulterior motives. These interruptions and pleadings did nothing to allay my irritability which at this time was considerable.

While all these events were taking place, the barricade across the street was steadily growing and consisted of as heterogeneous a collection of goods as might well be conjured up in a nightmare. It looked flimsy and frail in the extreme, due mainly to the nature of the contents. One of the men, in the hunt for barricade material, found a large coil of thin brass wire, the same as they use in the country for snaring rabbits. I almost jumped for joy when I saw it. Taking the coil I showed the men how to wind it round the various articles and finally fasten it round the poles and lamp standards at the street corners. This braced the whole contraption from end to end and converted what was an easily upset pile into a compact whole. It enabled me to take the men off barricading much earlier than I had expected.

By now it was fairly late in the night. The crowd had dwindled to a few drunks who seemed determined to make a night of it. I sent a scout down again to Amiens Street station telling him to approach it from the quay side. He brought back word that there were no British forces at all in Amiens Street. This good news allowed me to take the sentries off the door and windows and put them also on the work of barricading the building and boring holes in the party-walls between different premises.[67]

The idea of boring from one premises to another was part of Connolly's plan for holding the city. It was intended that the whole block would be bored in this way. This would remove the line of defence from the ground floor to the first floor. It would also enable rapid concentration at any threatened point. As a new premises was broken into in this way we had to descend to the ground floor and barricade the entrance doors and windows. If the windows were too big for barricading, as in fact all of them were, we had to fasten the entrance doors and block up the windows in such a way as to try to prevent the enemy's progress into the interior of the premises. In this way the ground floor would be cut off from the first floor which was the line we would fight on.

It was all really heart-breaking work. The masons who built these walls certainly knew their jobs as the masonry was as tough as the devil. There seemed to be no less than three party-walls adjoining the Imperial Hotel.

In order to try and speed up the work I sent a small party round to the Imperial Hotel with instructions to find out where the first party were boring by listening to the sound of the blows and then to start boring towards them. This proved not as simple as it sounded. It was an absolute puzzle to those on both sides of the wall. The sound of blows seemed to come from all parts of the wall at the same time.

After wasting a lot of precious time tapping and listening we at last concluded we were opposite each other and both sides slapped at it with vigour. In order not to entirely exhaust the men, and in view of the fact that there were no enemy in the vicinity, I had decided that this would be the last hole we would bore that night unless we got more reinforcements.

Eventually the men on the Imperial Hotel side began to come through to us but to our horror they came through a few feet below our ceiling! And on our side we were boring through a few feet below their floor! The floors in both premises were at different levels. This was what had made it so difficult to get opposite each other in the first instance.

When we got over our chagrin, we all squatted down on the floors and laughed. The innate sense of humour of the Dubliners came to our rescue. A search had then to be made for a ladder or a set of shop-steps to be put up from our floor to the hole under the ceiling so that we could pass through. It would be impossible to get quickly from one premises to another by this arrangement, so another hole would have to be punched first thing in the morning to bring us out on the floor on the Imperial side.[68]

Assembling all the men in one of the larger rooms I began the work of dividing them into sections and picking out the least fatigued for first sentry duty. After explaining the work of keeping watch and the method of reliefs through the rest of the night, I ordered all, except those picked for sentry duty, to get couches and mattresses and get what sleep they could.

Telling Crofts, whom I regarded as my second in command, to arrange for the men's breakfast at an early hour, and feeling refreshed after another cup of tea, I started up for the roofs again.

The great city was now strangely quiet. The occasional ribald shout of some belated drunk only seemed to accentuate the surrounding silence.

So ended the first day of the Rising.

Chapter 6
North Earl Street Command Post

Dreading that hour at which human life is reputed to be at its lowest ebb of vitality—and the favourite time of British attack—I had arranged to be called very early in the morning of the second day of the Rising. My first waking thought was for the GPO. There the lights were full on. Sentries were faintly visible at the windows, and shadowy figures were discernible passing to and fro. It was the only place within my entire range of vision which showed any signs of human life.

A strange feeling of personal isolation came over me. The men now directly associated with me were all strangers—with the sole exception of Gerald Crofts—and I was a stranger to them. It was impossible, at this early stage anyhow, to have that feeling of close comradeship which exists between soldiers who have been companions over a period of training.

I kept wondering how my own corps in Ferns were faring and how great generally was the state of confusion caused by the cancellation order.[69] Nor could I help wondering at the strange inactivity of the British authorities. Long hours had passed since we had seized the city; and with the solitary exception of the ridiculous charge of the mounted troops absolutely no hostile move had been made against us.

All British troops on city leave had returned to their barracks when the news of the seizure had become general knowledge, and there had been plenty of time to organise substantial sorties against us. One conclusion was that the element of surprise, which we had counted on, was even greater than we had originally hoped for. There was, of course, another reason: the extreme delicacy of the world war situation. The state of confusion in the minds of the British authorities must have been so great that they were awaiting fresh instructions from London before taking any overt measures.[70]

So the all-too-short night had passed in peace and quiet and another day of alarms, excitement and rumours dawned over the city. It was a new experience to watch the dawn finally break over the rooftops. How many of us might be stretched in death or wracked with agonising pains before another day was spent?

I made my way downstairs and telephoned an 'all quiet' report to general headquarters across the street. I announced that the Imperial Hotel was to be regarded as the command post headquarters. There were many reasons for this choice which it is not necessary to go into here. The principal one was the greater accommodation and comfort it afforded to the main body of my then little garrison.

Dublin appeared to come awake much later and more slowly than usual. There was none of the early morning bustle and clatter inseparable from the life of a great city. It was close to eight o'clock before there was any very noticeable movement of people and vehicles, and the latter were rather scarce.

I supposed everyone was in a state of uncertainty and indecision and had not yet recovered from the shock which our actions had given them. Small blame to them. It is one thing to read in the quiet of one's home of former risings and rebellions;

it is quite another thing to find oneself unexpectedly in the very midst of an actual rising, with the uncertainty of daily work looming and rations running short in the home. We hear all too seldom of the plain man's views on such matters.

The first job of the morning was to get all the garrison awake, except those who were last on sentry duty, and to see that they were washed and fed. There was no difficulty in rousing them; most of them were already awake and ready for action. Then a scout was again sent out towards Amiens Street station. Next I took a small party up to the roof. In the clearer light of day I pointed out to them the buildings most likely to be occupied by the enemy when he thought well of moving against us, and estimated the distance from our chimney pots and parapets to such buildings.

It was by now plain enough that the enemy did not contemplate any rash charges against our fortified positions—though fortification seems rather an inadequate word to use. His experience with the mounted troops would have taught him to have a certain amount of respect for us and caution as to his methods of approach.

There was a good deal of shouting and waving of hands between my post and the garrison in the GPO. In a quick checkup of my manpower I could find only one case of desertion during the night; and he a powerfully built man, to whom fighting should, on physical appearance anyhow, have come naturally if not from some deep well of patriotism.

Whilst the domestic chores were proceeding I descended to the street and made an outside inspection of the block. From the corner a narrow street ran down to a junction with Marlborough Street; and a narrow, traffic artery bisected the block of buildings. With enough men this lower block of buildings could be occupied by a detachment in the same way as the block fronting O'Connell Street. Such an occupation would certainly slow up and delay any direct attack on the general headquarters coming up from Amiens Street. But with my little garrison—which was now twenty men and four Cumann na mBan—this was out of the question. Indeed to hope to complete the boring and fortifying of the huge block before we were seriously attacked was also impossible.

However, in my own opinion a direct attack on our head-quarters, even from Amiens Street, was much more likely to develop from the quays than up North Earl Street. It was only in face of an immediate direct attack that I would, as Connolly did, direct the occupation of North Earl Street. Whilst an attack up this latter artery would be subject to our fire, an attack along the line of the quays could quickly and uninterruptedly reach the corner of O'Connell Street with almost unlimited possibilities of quick lateral development. However all that might be, we were now, for good or ill, tied to our present position.[71]

Having completed this survey—which would have been largely unnecessary by an officer well acquainted with the centre of the city—I stood at our barricade at the junction of North Earl Street and O'Connell Street and considered seriously the occupation and fortification of the opposite building. In fact I was under orders from Connolly to do so. But it was a physical impossibility at the moment. If I cut my scant force in two, the fire power of either would have been negligible. At that time, too, I was without the aid of a second officer to place in charge. I decided that unless I again got a direct order I would confine myself to making my present position as strong as possible. I had, up to this, only had a hasty cup of tea so I went and had a wash and breakfast.

Word was soon passed along to me that General Pearse had left the GPO and was coming across to us. I hastened to meet him. The door of our corner premises was just above the street barricade and we had left the door open for quick ingress and egress, with plenty of barricading piled in the hall. We both arrived at the footpath together. I saluted and expressed my pleasure at seeing him again. I invited him into the garrison, but assuring me that he was sure that everything was quite all right, he passed to the street barricade and just looked at it with a smile. It looked very frail so I drew his attention to the manner in which all the articles composing it were wired together and invited him to try and pull it asunder. Again he only smiled in his gentle way and made no attempt to do so.

We talked about the general position for a few moments and then I asked him if there was any news from Wexford. He looked directly at me and said that word had come in late the previous night that Wexford 'was out'. I expressed my satisfaction at the news, whereupon he turned away and went back to the GPO. I was left to conclude that the real purpose of his visit was to give me news of my Wexford comrades. It was typical of his innate kindness. It was the last time I was to see him in this life.

About an hour afterwards Connolly came striding briskly across the street to us. The men gave him a rousing cheer which he acknowledged with a quick wave of his hand. I was on the street at the time. He strode over to the barricade and immediately found fault with it. He said it was too small and too frail, and would not stop a charge. It certainly looked it. I invited him to try and knock it down. At once he seized the leg of a table, in the centre, and gave it a vigorous pull which did not budge it. I then pointed out the way the whole structure had been wired. This seemed to please him.[72]

I invited him also to inspect the garrison but on the plea that he had not the time he refused. I then gave him a brief verbal report as to the strength of my garrison, the state of arms and ammunition and my deductions as to the most likely quarter from which an assault on the GPO would develop. He listened attentively but made no comment.

He asked me if I intended to occupy the opposite corner. I said, no, and gave him my reasons, but added that if I got reinforcements enough in time I would certainly do so. Again he made no comment but stressed the importance of the post we held. I replied that I had already conveyed that to the members of the garrison. I took the liberty of suggesting the advisability of putting a garrison in one of the corner houses commanding the approach from the quays. He merely nodded at this, shook hands, wished us luck and took his departure back to the GPO. As with Pearse it was the last time I was ever to see him.

An incident which showed the amazing simplicity and sense of responsibility of the men occurred that morning. A spruce, stockily built young man wearing a blue nap-coat with a velvet collar came up to me, saluted, and asked permission to leave the garrison for an hour. The request struck me at once as a polite form of desertion. I asked him why he wanted time off. His answer left me gaping at him like a fool.

He said he was a foreman in a firm—which he named—and he had the keys with him. The boss and staff could not get in unless he turned up with the keys! He promised he would not be more than an hour away. When I recovered my wits I asked him did he not realise that our seizure of the city had brought all commercial life to a standstill. He replied that he supposed it had, but the keys were on his conscience and he would like to hand them over. Questioned as to why he did not leave the keys with the boss the previous Saturday, he replied that at the time he did not think of it and even if he had it might have aroused suspicion. Actually if he wished to desert there was no way I could prevent him; there were endless opportunities of slipping off unnoticed.

At any rate he did return within the hour. No man unexpectedly coming into a small fortune could have been more pleased than this rather simple-minded man was at having passed the keys to the boss. I have often wished I knew what the boss thought on that fateful morning of his employee's conscientiousness.

This incident was really typical of the attitude of the men. I well remember, when we were in the throes of fortifying the GPO, a young man coming to me and saying in an awe-struck tone that a till in one of the counters was packed with money. Sure enough it was full of notes and coins. This young man, obviously of the labouring class, had probably never earned more than thirty shillings a week in his life. Yet he had not touched a coin, though he could easily have stuffed his pockets and few, if anyone, would have been any the wiser. This led to a search of all the tills and the removal of their contents to a locked safe. The stories told, and printed, about men having been captured with their pockets stuffed to capacity with money were lies spread by a venomous enemy. There was not a word of truth in them.

Most of that second morning was spent in trying to improve our fortifications. One of the premises in the corner block was a merchant tailor's and the bales of tweed etc. came in very handy indeed.

I was very disappointed in the way the Citizen Army had been trained for their task.[73] They had a poor understanding of how to fortify a place. For example, when told to make loopholes in the front walls, they broke out holes far too large and had the widest ends facing the street. Fortunately they had saved the stones and bricks. It was, therefore, possible to remake the loopholes so that the narrowest opening faced the street and the widest end was on the inside. This gave the greatest degree of safety and the widest angle of fire.

By evening fairly large numbers of people had begun to congregate in O'Connell Street, but not in anything like the numbers of the previous evening. A big proportion of them were young women and chaps. These latter were the villains of the piece. There was a strong disposition on the part of the people to get into conversation with us. They really did not seem to understand what it was all about. Time and again we were most earnestly beseeched to go home before we were all killed!

On the other hand quite a number of young men still wanted to join up even though they had only the haziest idea of what it was all about. They seemed incapable of understanding that they really were in the midst of an Irish rebellion. Everyone, without exception, wanted to know if we expected to win. With a large grin we replied that we had already won. In a sense we spoke truer than we knew.

I do not know precisely when or how the looting started. It

was early evening, to the best of my recollection, and I think it was young chaps who started it, not so much in the form of looting as in a spirit of mischief. The first intimation I had was a sudden and lavish display of fireworks in the middle of O'Connell Street a short distance from our position.

It appears that a number of boys broke into Messrs Lawrence's, the toy shop. Carrying out armfuls of fireworks, they piled them up in the centre of the street and ignited them. They made a dramatic and impressive display and brought forth vociferous cheers. This, I believe, was sufficient to start wholesale looting in the centre of the city.[74]

Nothing brings out the base covetousness of human nature more than a period of disorder in a city. People of a normally honest social behaviour seem to break out in a rash of seizing other people's property even though the goods they steal are not of the least personal use to them. In the early part of the looting a young woman was talking to me on the footpath and trying to persuade me to go home before I was killed, when we both observed an aged man coming down the street towards us. He was bent over on a walking stick and a large white beard covered his chest.

Essentially he was of a poor but honest type. On his head was a tall shiny silk hat; around his shoulders was draped a lady's feather boa; and from his arm hung a flimsy lady's under-garment. He presented a most comical sight. There was not a smile on his wrinkled features and he seemed bent on making his way home with his loot.

'Look at this old reprobate', shouted my companion. As he came abreast of us she yelled at him: 'It's at home you should be saying your prayers, you old fool.'

Without a word the old man took off the feather boa and handed it to the young woman, who snatched it angrily out of his hand, threw it on the footpath and then kicked it into the gutter saying heatedly as she did so: 'You want me to be as bad as yourself, you old reprobate!'

He had not gone far before a youngster flung a missile at him, hit the tall hat fair and square, and tumbled it off his head. He passed on out of our sight still tenaciously clutching the lady's undergarment. This was only one of many outlandish incidents, each more ridiculous and farcical than the other.[75]

This looting was bad enough, but when the mob took to setting the looted premises on fire to cover their depredations the position became dangerous in the extreme. Some time about mid-evening a riotous gang broke into a shoe shop in the very centre of my position in O'Connell Street. Having looted the shop window they managed to set fire to it, and we had to threaten to open fire on them to clear them off.

I would have made an example of one or two of the looters but for the fact that we had received the strictest instructions from Connolly himself that we were not to interfere in any way with any civilian unless they made a direct assault on our person. I regarded the looting of a premises in my position and then setting fire to it as a very direct form of assault; but Connolly's order was explicit not to interfere unless personally assaulted. There was nothing for it but to obey. An aggravating part of the looting was that many looters showed no disposition to carry away the loot, but contented themselves with flinging it out the windows and then kicking it around the street. One could understand and to an extent sympathise with people, ill-clad and probably hungry, being tempted beyond endurance and carrying the loot home. But this insensate passion for wanton destruction was maddening.[76]

In the end I tried out a plan suggested by one of the garrison, all of whom were very angry at this brazen attempt to burn us out. I yelled at the top of my voice that anyone attempting to loot or light fires in our vicinity would be shot. If they wanted to loot they would have to do so somewhere else. This word was relayed by the crowd, after which we were left in comparative peace.

I cannot let the recording of these events pass without paying a well-deserved tribute to the Dublin fire brigade. All that evening and night they were being called to fires in O'Connell Street and they uncomplainingly responded to every call. They continued to render this service until some time on Wednesday when we had occasion to call them to a fire which had broken out rather mysteriously in our vicinity. When the call went through the fire brigade replied that they were prohibited from answering any more calls from O'Connell Street and that the British authorities had told them that there would be many more fires in O'Connell Street before they were finished with us.

Except for continual looting and some isolated fires there were no alarms in our area. A fairly large number of people continued to stroll about as if nothing untoward was happening. There was a good deal of traffic between our post and the GPO, many of the men, when off duty, seeking permission to visit relatives and friends in the post office. There was no good reason for refusing this permission so long as they did not stay too long or upset the routine of duty.

A good many passers-by seemed to resent our street barricade when they found it impeded them from going from O'Connell Street down North Earl Street or entering from the latter into the main thoroughfare. Some of them even had the temerity to demand that we leave a pass way! No one, of course, was allowed to touch or interfere with the barricade in any way. Nearly all of them accepted the situation with good grace when the purpose of the barricade was explained to them. After all, they had only a few yards to traverse, up or down, to get a turning that led to their route.

Shortly after ten o'clock that night an impetuous young lady came striding briskly across O'Connell Street towards our corner. I happened to be standing in our doorway as she approached. Seeing her head for the barricade, which was about six or seven feet high, I called out that she could not pass that way. She stopped, stared at me in an obviously very hostile manner and then ejaculated the one word: 'Why?'

'I should think it's plain enough', I replied shortly. 'The street is blocked and no one is allowed to touch the barricade.'

'And what right have you to block up the street and prevent decent people from going home?', she demanded.

'No one is preventing you from going home. All you have to do is walk a few, a very few yards down the street and you will have a clear course to your home. Under the circumstances that is not asking too much of anyone.'

It was all no use really. She was of the bull-headed bossy type and was bent on having her own way. As her voice was continually rising in shrill angry tones, a little crowd of the idle curious had gathered at the opposite corner.

'I have gone home this way all my life and I'm going home this way tonight. I'd like to see anyone try to stop me.'

'Well', I retorted, 'we have the means of stopping you if we think fit.'

'I am going home that way and no other way.'

Some of the garrison had by now gathered near me and one of them suggested removing her by force but I was against it. The emotions of a crowd are about the most fickle thing in the world. Besides I knew she could do no real damage to the barricade, but if she established a precedent we would certainly have to interfere or the barricade would simply disintegrate.

Without further ado she seized the nearest article to her hand. As she did so I warned: 'You may break your neck.'

'I don't care if I do. It's my own neck.' Then with true feminine logic she added, 'If I do it will be your fault.'

A man who seeks to argue with a woman once she has made up her mind is a fool. So we let her at it. As she began to climb over the barricade the crowd gave her a little cheer. One man who apparently knew her called out her name and a word of encouragement. She turned towards him angrily, obviously intent on giving him, too, a bit of her mind. But the sudden jerk round was fatal to her precarious balance and she slipped back to the ground, giving what was in those days an unusual display of legs and petticoat. This mishap brought a loud roar of laughter from the crowd. This made her really furious and she vented her ill-feeling impartially on all and sundry. She again essayed the climb, but as she crossed the top she stepped on some article that seemed to give way under her weight. Losing her balance she plunged headlong to the pavement, her legs waving grotesquely in the air. Again, the crowd roared and clapped their hands. Picking herself up she continued on her way, calling out invectives over her shoulder until she passed out of sight and sound.

Repeated scoutings were made to Amiens Street station without any evidence of the enemy being discovered. This gave me more time and confidence. And so the weary, if sometimes amusing, day passed into silent night without a single challenge to our supremacy.

Chapter 7
The Fight Begins

The second night passed without anything happening to disturb the peace and security of our position. The boring of walls and the inside fortification had gone on to a late hour. High spirits and a general air of confidence—desirable qualities in those who had never yet heard the close and sinister whine of an angry bullet—were apparent in the members of the garrison.

Outside the city had become quiet. The last of the idle curious had taken himself off. From the rooftops, only the sudden, momentary flare-up of some still smouldering fire was a reminder that we stood in the centre of a city of death and destruction. From down beyond the harbour came the hoot of a ship's siren, speaking importantly of the great needs of peace and commerce. There could be little doubt that the sleep of the great city was an uneasy one. Problems of food and wages and work must have been agitating many minds.

Until I stood on the rooftops after midnight I never realised what uneasy birds seagulls were. They seemed to have no settled regime of repose, like the other members of the feathered tribes, but kept on wheeling, dipping and rising throughout the darkening hours, calling continuously to one another with their shrill cries.

The morning of the third day of the Rising dawned roseate and glorious. To country-trained eyes it spoke of another day of sunshine and warmth. Again the city was slow to come to life. There was much less bustle and scurry than on the previous morning. It seemed as if the city was reluctant to begin the services of human life and had resigned itself to that state of inevitable chaos which it could not now avoid.

During the course of the previous day some reinforcements had come in dribs and drabs. They came in every case directly from the GPO. There the tricolour still floated lazily in the morning breeze and the Proclamation made a brave splash of white on the wall. By midday the garrison had been increased to about forty men. Many of the latecomers were Volunteers and again they were strangers to me.[77] But we had no reserve of ammunition and the American single-barrel shotguns were proving a curse. There were several near escapes of death from them. If a man let the butt thump on the ground the shot went off at once. This happened several times with men getting through the holes in the walls in passing from one premises to another. I had to circulate an order that all shotguns were to be kept strictly unloaded. In the early morning there was still a certain amount of comradely traffic between the post and the GPO, but there did not seem to be the same eagerness to visit pals as on the previous day.

Reports began to reach us. Skimpy and inconclusive, not much reliance could be placed upon them, and certainly no valid picture of the situation outside of our area could be erected upon them. Some of our outposts, particularly on the south side of the city, had been driven in or withdrawn. News reached us of the great fight at Ashbourne and was a good tonic. We had known of the failure to seize Dublin Castle. We now learned that advance elements of the enemy had penetrated as far as Great Brunswick Street and were also located in the grounds of Trinity College.[78] News of the heroic fight put up by a mere handful of Volunteers at Mount Street Bridge put great heart into the men. On the whole there was little news calculated to damp the ardour. There was a tendency to sing and whistle and even to indulge in some rough horse-play.

Between eight and nine o'clock there was a burst of gunfire and exploding shells in our rear. All hands bounded to their posts. Word came down from the roof that the firing was somewhere about the Custom House. At long last the enemy had swung into action. The period of waiting, of funny incidents and looting, was over. Nevertheless there were still pedestrians knocking about. Nothing seemed to damp the avid curiosity of some people.

Then, quite suddenly, bursts of rifle fire came in short spatters. Enemy snipers were coming into action. It was a little difficult to locate them. When we did, short bursts were sent in reply. Some of the men were proving to be remarkably good shots. The Howth Mauser, used from a rest, was also proving a remarkably accurate weapon. Odd hours of the previous day had been spent in picking out the most likely buildings for the enemy to occupy and estimating the distance to them from us. We were now reaping the benefit of that precaution.

––––

Before I pass to the recording of the actual fighting around our area there are some points I should like to clear up. Quite a flood of fiction has been published about alleged happenings during the course of the Rising and many of these hoary old lies are still going the rounds. That journalists and journals should revel in exaggerations and stories in a welter of 'hot news' is understandable. What is not understandable nor excusable is that these should be gathered up and preserved permanently in book form, thus misleading future historians and researchers. It has been stated:

> Twelve o'clock in the day was the hour fixed for the beginning of the operations, and at that time, or shortly afterwards, bodies of armed Sinn Féiners quietly entered the buildings to which they had been assigned, turned out the occupants and took possession. Anyone who resisted was promptly shot.

This is absolutely untrue. No one was shot in this way; and there were positive orders to the contrary.

Again:

> Provisions were taken at the point of the bayonet.

Nothing was taken at the point of the bayonet. Bayonets were scarce indeed. All commandeering was done on duly-signed requisitions, which the people concerned were entitled to hold and use to claim compensation later. As far as was practical all commandeering was from wealthy firms who could afford to wait for their legitimate compensation.

Again:

> Liberty Hall was strongly held . . . Wednesday morning the Admiralty steamer, *Helga*, came up the Liffey and bombarded

Liberty Hall, the headquarters of the Citizen Army. Owing to the loop-line bridge intervening between the ship and Liberty Hall, direct fire could not be brought to bear on the building.

The ship's gunners, however, dropped shells on the hall, the roof and interior was destroyed by bursting shells, but the outer shell of the building was not much injured by fire. The garrison escaped before the bombardment commenced. Artillery brought from Trinity College also shelled Liberty Hall.

Liberty Hall was not strongly held. Nor was it then the head-quarters of the Citizen Army. To my personal knowledge it was evacuated by all combatant members on the previous Monday. I have no doubt that on Wednesday many old and non-combatant members of the Irish Transport and General Workers Union were in and hanging around their beloved hall. Where else had they to go? Their leaders, sons, relatives and comrades were already in the GPO. All this shelling from land and water was directed against a vacant building. If Liberty Hall had been strongly held there would have been no necessity for Connolly to have ordered the hasty occupation of North Earl Street, as Liberty Hall would have had to be dealt with before any advance could have been made along this route against the GPO. The British could not afford to leave a strongly held position intact on their flank. No, Liberty Hall was shelled and destroyed simply because it was the home of the Transport Union and the Citizen Army.

Yet again:

All the corner houses commanding the approaches [to the GPO] were garrisoned by snipers, who were hidden behind sandbags. Kelly's ammunition shop at the corner of Bachelor's Walk, and Hopkins' jewellery shop at the corner of Eden Quay were held in this way in great strength. Other houses on each side of Lower Sackville Street [now O'Connell Street] and particularly those at the four corners of Abbey Street, were garrisoned in like manner.[79]

I only wish it were true. There were no garrisons at the four corners of Abbey Street. The fight might have been different if there had been. And, it is made to appear that 'hidden behind sandbags' was contemptible and cowardly, whereas sandbags have always been used in military defence. In our case there were no sandbags, and the fortifications that were erected had to be composed of such materials as happened to be found in the buildings. In nearly every instance these were of a flimsy and insecure nature.

Even the absurd charge of the mounted troops down O'Connell Street on Monday is made to appear in a false light, in an effort to throw discredit on the forces of the Republic. It was alleged that the troop of lancers were escorting some wagons of ammunition from the North Wall to the magazine in Phoenix Park, passing up Eden Quay and Bachelor's Walk in entire ignorance of what was taking place. This may well have been so.

But it was further alleged that 'some of them' returned to the city and came into O'Connell Street from the north end. As soon as they got in front of the GPO they were met with a volley from the occupants of that building.

The shots came for the most part from men who had got on the roof, from which position they had a great advantage over the Lancers.

It would be extremely difficult to imagine anything more childish than this story. We are asked to believe that 'some' lancers, engaged in escort duty, casually rode back into the heart of the city as if they were veritable 'innocents abroad', and that they were shot at in a most cowardly manner. If this story were to be accepted as true then a poor view must be taken of the state of discipline in the British army.[80]

Space prohibits me from traversing all the absurd stories about this period; but I trust I have quoted enough to illustrate the extreme caution with which this type of 'history' must be approached.

———

Quite suddenly we were startled by a burst of machine-gun fire which seemed reasonably close to us. A discussion arose as to exactly where it had come from. Some of the men on sentry contended it had come from Kelly's at the corner of Bachelor's Walk. I was very sceptical of this. Up to that moment no report had been received of a new occupation at this point, and I felt sure that the enemy could not have got so close unobserved, since our windows were not for an instant without sentries on the watch.

While I was staring intently at this corner, there was a longer and stronger burst of machine-gun fire. It came from the corner window of the first floor of Kelly's, and the bursts were directed down the quays towards the Custom House. It seemed clear that a machine-gun of ours was located there. This deepened the mystery as I had neither seen nor heard of a machine-gun being amongst our equipment. There were, in all, three bursts of machine-gun fire from this point, after which the post must have been vacated as we did not observe any further firing from it.

So far as we were concerned the British attack had begun. At first it was spasmodic and intermittent. They were feeling out our positions, encouraging us, so to speak, to return their fire and thus reveal our positions and possibly our strength to them. As the morning advanced the tempo of the attack rose. There was a great volume of rifle fire and frequent bursts of machine-gun fire. It was all from buildings and fairly distant. There was no sign of a direct assault upon us. If such a form of attack did not develop then the time and labour we had spent erecting street barricades would be wasted.

By degrees the men of the garrison became very quick at picking out the location of enemy posts and attacking them with rifle fire. A surprising feature of this duel was that as soon as we located a post and sent a few shots into it, the enemy quitted that point and moved to another close by. I made continual rounds of our firing positions, warning the men to fire slowly and only when they were reasonably sure of their targets. One could not estimate how long this form of distant duelling might continue and having regard to our scant supplies of ammunition it was imperative that supplies be carefully husbanded. In this way the morning merged into forenoon without much damage or change of tactics on either side.

After midday, however, machine-gun fire became pronounced and the volume of rifle fire increased considerably. The enemy obviously considered that his advance elements had uncovered our pattern and had moved up reinforcements. While the main enemy fire was directed against the GPO, we had been discovered and bullets began to whiz and zip around us, many of them coming in through the windows.

Fortunately they were all high shots and no damage or casualties were caused. The distance and the high trajectory of the firing had this advantage for us: it accustomed the men to the somewhat nerve-wracking rattle of machine-guns and the whine and smack of bullets without producing any apparent tendency to panic from the effects of actual casualties. In addition to warnings about husbanding ammunition it was now necessary to warn the men to keep down under cover as they had been instructed. This meant continuous activity and climbing through the holes in the walls became somewhat fatiguing.

I had a great deal of unnecessary trouble with one Citizen Army man stationed at a corner window in the Pillar Cafe. He was a tall, lanky man, with a big walrus moustache, aged about fifty and armed with a Mauser. He had what seemed to be an instinctive habit of sticking his head out of the window every time he fired a shot or a bullet zoomed off the wall near him. He had been warned several times of the unnecessary danger of this habit.

On one occasion when I was kneeling beside him a bullet smashed into the window sash just where his head had been a second or so before. He danced with rage, stuck his head out again, but quickly drew it back and said apologetically to me: 'Yer right, sir.'

I asked him if he could locate the spot from which this shooting was coming. 'There's a so-and-so down there in Trinity College an' I'll get him if it's the last thing I do. It's him that nearly got me that time.'

Fearing that he would stick his head out again I made him abandon the window, lie down on the floor and, using the loophole under it, point out to me the position he had referred to.

A corner of a building in Trinity jutted out to the left and gave a clear if limited view of our front line of wall. Focusing my glasses, I found an occupied window on, I think, the first floor.

Taking the man's rifle I told him to fix his hat in an angle of the window as soon as I gave him the word. Being a good shot I stretched out on the floor and got the window in Trinity lined up in my sights.

'Now', I called, and the instant the hat went up a bullet smashed into the side of our window. I fired at once, but must have missed as a return shot came immediately. After a brief exchange of shots with the sniper in Trinity there came a lull from that quarter. This did not mean that I had inflicted a casualty. Possibly the other had grown canny. He had not the same advantage of a loophole that I had. As I could not remain too long in the one spot I returned the rifle to my companion and told him to follow my example and fire from the loophole.[81]

Our task consisted mainly in locating snipers and machine-gun nests. When such a nest was discovered and a few rifle shots were sent against it, it moved to some other window, floor or building and the hunt had to begin all over again. It was a form of deadly hide and go seek. In this we had the advantage as we possessed loopholes and a certain amount of cover at the windows.

Sometimes, try as we might, we could not discover the exact position of a machine-gun. There was some obstruction to our view. As the phone was still operating satisfactorily we phoned the location of such a gun to the GPO, as accurately as we could. The GPO, finding themselves in a similar difficulty, phoned us and asked us to try and attend to the nest. In this way the duel went on continuously without, it must be said, very much damage to either side.

In the forenoon tragedy and comedy followed each other in quick succession. Quite suddenly a small man, wearing mole-skin trousers, a blue reefer coat and a peaked cap—obviously a navvy—came out of Henry Street by the post office corner into O'Connell Street. He had barely crossed the footpath when he suddenly sprawled onto his face in the gutter and lay still. Immediately there was a screech and a woman, her shawl streaming out behind her, dashed out of Henry Street and flung herself on top of the figure. At first we thought that she too had been shot; but she began to shout and caress the prone figure. Next a small party of Volunteers came out of the Henry Street entrance, gathered up the prone figure and bore it away, the woman following.

We were so intent on the tragedy that we were all taken by surprise to observe another strange figure coming down the centre of O'Connell Street. Where he had come out of we did not know. But there he was, careering down the middle of the street, amidst a torrent of machine-gun and rifle fire. A very tall, lanky man, he was wearing a bowler hat with a light, duskish-coloured shower coat swung open from his shoulders. He was most gloriously drunk, travelling at a pace that was extremely erratic, being a jogtrot one moment and a halting stagger the next. He was singing at the top of his voice, gesticulating violently with his arms, living and moving in a hilarious world of his own.

At the time this apparition—for such it seemed to us at first glance—appeared, O'Connell Street and the front of the GPO were being pasted with machine-gun and rifle fire. Bullets were zipping and ricocheting off walls and paving sets. Yet this extraordinary figure was oblivious to it all. We thought every drunken stagger was a hit, but the next instant he would begin his jogtrot again. Every second we expected to see him go down riddled with bullets. He simply could not escape. But he did.

As soon as we recovered from our surprise we all began shouting at the drunk to get out of there and into cover. But he paid no more attention to us than if we were so many flies buzzing about him in the warm sunshine. Some of the men, pitying his condition and danger, wanted to go out and drag him to safety but I forbade it. As far as we could observe him— we were all in crouching positions—he continued his weird career down O'Connell Street in safety. It was a miracle of preservation.

About the middle of the afternoon extremely heavy, concentrated machine-gun and rifle fire blazed up from some position in our left rear. It was not directed at us but at the GPO. I felt it presaged an assault. Going to the phone to report to the commander in the post office I found the instrument dead. It was essential to get into communication again. Any failure to break up the machine-gun nests would mean that the cordon of fire and shells would be drawn tighter and closer about us. Every effort had to be made to keep it at a distance.

Writing out a despatch, I called for a volunteer to take it across to the GPO. At once every man in the room stepped forward. The senior lady of the Cumann na mBan group was in the room at the time. She too volunteered. When I rejected her offer she coolly informed me that they were short of bandages, splints, etc., so that in any case she would have to accompany the messenger. I replied that the messenger would bring back the supplies if she indented for them but she countered this by saying that he would not know where to go and would lose valuable time. It was evident she was determined on going no matter what I said. So far there were no casualties in the garrison; but as we were now hotly contested, and with streams of bullets coming in the windows and ricocheting around in all directions, we could not expect to be immune much longer. It would not do to be short of first aid kit.

The lady was not in uniform and wore what was called a 'hobble' skirt, or what looked like one to me. She would certainly need the full and free use of her limbs when she got out in front. With her permission, therefore, we slit her skirt from just above the knee, thus giving her freedom of movement. Taking her down to the hallway and removing the barricade at the door, we told her to rush straight across. She did so and much to our relief arrived safely. In a very short time she reappeared in the post office doorway. Putting down her head and with her arms laden with supplies, she broke into a headlong rush across the street and made it. She was a very brave lady.

But the problem of communication remained. Despatch runners could not be sent across the street every time I had a report to make. Enemy snipers would quickly observe the movement, interpret it correctly, wait for the next one and pick him off like game on the wing. Sending reports over by semaphore might be possible, though few Volunteers or Citizen Army were really proficient at it. Certainly none in my garrison. Besides men semaphoring would have to stand in front of the window and be so exposed that their careers would be short.

As I pondered the problem the idea of pitching a weighted ball of twine across the tram wires and on towards the GPO occurred to me. One or two of the men said that they could pitch such a ball right across the street and into the window of the GPO! This boast brought a laugh. A hunt began in the shops below for balls of twine and weights. They were quickly found. The despatch was wrapped round the weight which was secured in the centre of the ball of twine. The most boastful then took it, ran out a generous supply of loose twine, gave the ball a few vigorous twirls around his head and pitched with all his might. An ironic cheer arose. The ball of twine barely cleared our own footpath.

An effort by another man reached nearly midway across the street. Finally a ball was pitched with such skill and power that it landed beyond the centre of the street and did a roll almost to the channel beside the footpath on the post office side. We had to wave and sign to those in the GPO to come out and get the ball of twine. Eventually a man darted out, seized the ball and with a single throw pitched it in through the post office window.

The message inside merely said that the phone had gone dead and that we wanted to re-establish communication. We asked them to pass the twine round some fixture and pitch it back to us. The ball came sailing out of the post office window, but, alas, it barely cleared the tram lines and did not roll an inch. Instantly Gerald Crofts dashed downstairs, seized the ball, ran to the footpath and pitched it through our window. The two ends of the twine were knotted together and so we had re-established our line of communication by 'cablegram'.

Going up to the roof once more, I was told that the most troublesome machine-gun fire came from somewhere to our left rear and was not observable from our post. Writing out a report I returned to the 'cable room' and ordered the report to be tied to the twine and pulled across. Returning a few minutes later I was told the contraption would not do. I was shown a tin canister which had been attached to the twine. A bullet hole through it was less than half an inch below the twine itself. A little higher and the shot would have left us again without means of communication. I told them to take off the canister and simply tie the message around the twine in a way unlikely to be detected by the enemy.

At the same time the hail of bullets in this area was such that I would not have been surprised if the 'cable' was cut half a dozen times by accident. But this simple twine arrangement continued to work satisfactorily throughout the remainder of our occupation.

I was standing to one side of the big window in the Imperial Hotel surveying the scene through my glasses. We were still being harassed by the sniper in Trinity. Suddenly there was a terrific detonation quite close. Smoke, flame and debris belched out of a building in Prince's Street. Seeing it, the men gave a rousing cheer. The shell, fired at the GPO, had hit the *Freeman's Journal* editorial offices and works. This paper had been an out-and-out supporter of the Irish Parliamentary Party, and its destruction instead of the GPO was taken as a good omen. Just then I was called to the North Earl Street end of our position.

It was my old friend of the walrus moustache. He pointed to an open window on the opposite side of the street, towards the Parnell monument. He reported that a bald-headed man had appeared at this window, looked out and waved a coloured handkerchief, after which the shell came along. I looked at him sharply to see if he had been drinking, then said it could not be. No shells, so far, had been directed at our position and Baldy was on the wrong side of the street to act as an artillery observation against the GPO.

'Right side or wrong side, I'm telling ye, every time he waves his hankie a shell explodes somewhere. I'm after firing at the so-and-so several times, but he's a game old cock, and he ducks out again as large as life, just like a jack-in-the-box. I'd like to put a stop to his antics.'

Replying to questions, the sentry said that no one had been observed at any of these windows since early Tuesday morning, and all the premises had the appearance of being deserted until this 'so-and-so came poking his head out and waving his hankie'.

Certainly no one had any business engaging in this peculiar practice in the existing situation. I could not bring myself to believe that he was an observation officer. The fact that he was dressed in 'civvies' really meant nothing.

However, while I stood watching the window the large, bald head suddenly appeared, looked swiftly up and down the street, gave a flick to a large coloured handkerchief or cloth and ducked back again. Sure enough within less than half a minute a shell burst well to the rear of the post office. Judging by sound the explosion must have been well down behind the post office towards the quays. This was too regular to be coincidental, still I could not follow what system of observation and direction was being used. It was a new one on me.

Baldy would have to be shifted and that quickly. One incendiary shell fired at our position, under his direction, would wipe us out very quickly indeed. We had only escaped so far because of the urgent desire on the part of the enemy to knock out the GPO. It was necessary to put him physically out of action, if possible, because if sufficiently exasperated he might turn the gun on us, despite anxiety to get our general headquarters.

Taking his Mauser from the sentry, I stretched out on the floor at the loophole and brought the window into the line of sights. After perhaps six or seven minutes, the head popped out again, took a swift look up and down, and flicked the handkerchief. I waited to get the head dead on the sights, and just as I squeezed the trigger he popped back down. I had missed. But I had the pleasure of seeing a large mirror hanging on the opposite wall go into smithereens. It was dead in line with where the head had been.

I waited patiently for what must have been ten minutes but there was no reappearance of the head. Returning the rifle, I gave instructions for a close watch to be kept for similar cases of signalling. I then continued making my rounds.

This first day of fighting had been nerve-wracking for men who had never before come under hostile fire. The vicious rattling of machine-guns was particularly unsettling. Yet the men stood up to it with remarkable sang-froid. So far we had not a single casualty and the enemy had kept to a respectable distance. It was a day of snatching a mouthful of food between alarms, a day of catnapping rests, a day of continual vigilance.

In this way the day ended and night came.

Chapter 8
Problems and their Solutions

I do not know any more hateful expression in the English language than 'I told you so'. Yet under certain circumstances it is capable of great personal consolation of a negative kind. Certainly it gave me a degree of consolation several times throughout Wednesday as I paused on my peregrinations of my post, looked abroad over the now rapidly developing situation, and sought to work out in my mind an evaluation of the possibilities, including alternatives.

That which I had sought to impress on the general staff time and again, and once on General Connolly, was now obviously taking place before our eyes. The British, consciously or unconsciously, were adopting our plan. They were occupying strategic points, possibly throwing up barricades, and drawing a ring of fire tighter and tighter around us. We had no effective reply to that plan. The longer we remained fighting as we were the more desperate our position became. We were simply in a ring of steel and fire from which there were only two avenues of escape—death or surrender. I do not think a single man of the garrison feared death. They all dedicated their lives to the service of Ireland and death in the service had no terrors for them. But surrender was hateful.

However what was more hateful was the prospect of a quick

defeat to our efforts in arms to serve our beloved land. To put up a prolonged resistance that would appeal to the fighting instincts of our race and thereby rouse our people out of the apathy they had sunk into under constitutionalism—that, I believe, was very close to all our hearts. Now that hope was fast fading into another chapter of failure. Once more an Irish 'rebellion' was about to be squelched in a holocaust of blood, fire and tears.

Such were the thoughts that kept running through my mind that Wednesday night as the hours passed by. I knew not the moment they might be ended by the swushing arrival of an incendiary shell in our block. Fortunately for us, these grim possibilities had been present in my mind from the beginning. As a result we had rehearsed a method of evacuation, as best we could in the circumstances, in the event of our coming under direct shell fire.

Ordinary shell fire which blows out a section of the building is bad enough, but it generally leaves a marginal foothold from which an effective resistance may be maintained. But an incendiary shell, which would set the whole block blazing, could only be met in one way—instant evacuation. That situation could confront us at any moment.[82] That it had not done so before now was solely due to the fact that the enemy was obviously concentrating on the GPO because it was the headquarters of the provisional government of the Irish Republic. He wanted a quick finish.

My orders had been to hold the post to the last man. Beyond that they did not go. Beyond that I considered I was free to do the best I could under the circumstances. A raging fire would certainly cancel out the post.

What was the best course under such circumstances? That was the problem. I was handicapped by lack of an intimate knowledge of the back lanes, back streets, and those queer and unexpected byways and alleys which are common to every city. Had it been in the country I would have been in my natural element and it would have been possible to give an enemy unacquainted with the terrain a really tough time. What then was to be done when the fatal incendiary arrived, as I felt certain it would?

Should we stick it out and be burned to death? That would have been a blind and ignorant obedience to orders, and besides, the men could not humanly be expected to obey such a crazy order. Should we simply evacuate into the opposite corner of North Earl Street and continue the fight from there? At best it would only mean a respite of a few hours. Should we evacuate to the GPO, from whence we had come? Such was the intensity of the fire directed at the GPO building on this Thursday morning that the evacuation of about forty men and four ladies across the width of O'Connell Street would be hazardous in the extreme. And what real benefit would we be to that garrison when we got there? They already had a strong garrison, by which I mean such numbers of poorly trained men as the few officers could be expected to handle. When it was hit with an incendiary the addition of my garrison would really only add to the difficulty of evacuation. The building was already the object of artillery fire. That it was erratic and uncertain up to now made no real difference. Sooner or later they would find the range and then there would be no alternative but evacuation.

It was a problem that I had to try to solve by myself. I could not discuss it with any members of the garrison. To have done so would have been psychologically bad. The simplest solution was to evacuate to the opposite corner of North Earl Street. The operation would be comparatively safe, but it did not appeal to me. We could, of course, have continued to duplicate this move if we had to. But such 'Jack Rabbit' tactics would only result in the total destruction of the business centre of the city with no real military gain accruing to us.

I felt if I could slip my little force through the British lines, which did not seem to be a continuous line to our rear, and if we could reach open country, we could achieve some real purpose. By attacking from the rear we could well bring some relief to the hard-pressed GPO. The British would have to reverse some of their forces to deal with us. We might even have a chance of attacking an artillery post and knocking the gun out of action.

Dreams? Well, perhaps, but it seemed to me that this was our best shot, if we were to remain in the fight to any advantage. Two things were necessary: the cover of darkness to enable us to slip through the lines; and some guide who had an intimate knowledge of the back streets and alleyways of the city.

These were the thoughts and ideas with which I greeted the dawn that Thursday morning. Eventually I decided to take the men into my confidence. I felt that their courage and staunchness had entitled them to it. Of course I could not call the whole garrison together and harangue them on the subject. So I picked out a few who had shown a quicker disposition to grasp the military angles than the others. Quietly I put my evaluation of the situation before them: that if we could get behind the British lines we could possibly make some real contribution towards altering the general pattern of the fight. I concluded by saying frankly that it was more or less a forlorn hope, and being so I would not make it a matter of discipline. As their lives were now at stake I would leave the decision to them. I then asked them to go and talk the matter over with the men and to let me know the result.

There was virtually a unanimous decision to abide by my orders. The only exception was a young civil servant who preferred to make an effort to rejoin the GPO. He had a close pal in the GPO and wished to be with him at the end. He was the only one of my garrison whom I could never trace afterwards.

This decision was a tremendous relief to me. I had risked a split in the opinion of the garrison and had waited on the decision with trepidation. It brought home to me, too, the degree of confidence the men had in my judgement—and there is no greater comfort to a commander be he professional or insurgent.

Now it was time to prepare for our possible new adventure. We could not quit our position until absolutely compelled to. And if an incendiary shell arrived in broad daylight we could only cross North Earl Street and do the best we could from there until darkness came. I enquired what was the nearest open country to our rear and was promptly told Fairview. To me it was no more than a name. Next I enquired if there was any man who had a really intimate knowledge of the city byways from our position to Fairview. A man was brought to me who claimed to know the city as well as he knew the back of his hand.[83]

A typical Dubliner he was aged about sixty, low of stature and stocky of build. Dressed in a navy blue suit and wearing a bowler hat, he certainly did not look the part of a revolutionary, but much more like a man who spent his days at his trade and his evenings in the 'local'. However, he was active, quick of mind and as far as I could judge intelligent. At the back of my mind there lay the wish for the open country and a poacher for a guide.

Having gone over the details and impressed on him the necessity of using back lanes and alleyways, I told him to assume that the order to evacuate had been given and to tell me exactly how he would guide us to our destination.

He said at once that if we broke in at a particular door on the opposite side of North Earl Street we would have a clear passage right through the block to Marlborough Lane. He then detailed other lanes and alleys which were only so many names to me. But it was excellent, the very thing I had hoped to find.

Taking him up to the North Earl Street corner I made him point out the exact door on the opposite side which he had referred to. I instructed him that the moment the evacuation order was given he was to make his way to me and to stick to my side no matter what happened. The success or failure of our new adventure would depend mainly on his guidance. He seemed greatly pleased by this responsibility. Perhaps in the course of the occupation and fighting he had unduly felt the weight of the years and his lack of military training; but now the account was being balanced out for him. Nothing increases the morale of an elderly man more than the knowledge that his usefulness is still far from coming to an end.

Now the order of evacuation had to be explained to the men and the resting reliefs given discreet practice in orderly evacuation. This was by no means as easy as it sounds. It was impossible to foretell where the infernal incendiary would come dropping in. The best route was through Fagan's public house;

but this was as likely to be the first place hit. If that happened then the evacuation would have to be from the Imperial Hotel into the narrow street running parallel with it, then through the traffic lane bisecting the block of buildings and so into North Earl Street. This route would take more than three times as long as going through Fagan's, but it would be under cover.[84]

The main thing was to ensure beforehand that everyone understood the precise direction of the evacuation order— which would be either 'Evacuate by Fagan's' or 'Evacuate by the Imperial'— and that everyone would move in the given direction at once and in an orderly fashion.

This meant that the resting reliefs had to be exercised in both routes. This was frequently interrupted by calls from various fighting points and the necessity to rush extra men to these spots to increase the firing power. Fortunately we had so far suffered no casualties. This was due to two things: insistence from the beginning on the men taking proper advantage of cover and the fact that except from Trinity College we were largely sheltered from direct fire.

Our primitive communications twine was still operating efficiently and well. So far as could be gathered from the rather skimpy reports that came to us over the twine from the GPO, it appeared that everywhere we were still holding our original occupation points. This in itself was highly satisfactory and encouraging, and such reports were always circulated round the garrison. Nonetheless, there could be no doubting that we were being hemmed in, and even on the basis of available ammunition the end was in sight. A breakthrough, even on a small scale, seemed the only way to breach the ring, halt the pressure and gain a valuable breathing space. It might be even possible to open an avenue for the GHQ, though having regard to the heavy fire directed against it, this was very doubtful.

In a fairly long report to the general staff I set out my intentions in the event of being burned out and had it pulled across. I received no comment on the report and concluded that in the event of being burned out we were free to act on our own initiative.[85]

I am aware that this may seem an example of being wise after the event. But it must not be forgotten that the Volunteers had been in existence for some time and that this question of operations and alternatives had been discussed from every angle. Time and again I had gone over plans and counterplans for the Wexford brigades. Moreover, J. J. O'Connell and myself had on various occasions discussed both local and general plans as well as various alternatives. We had assumed certain contingencies—such as the one we now found ourselves in—and argued out various solutions. It was not, therefore, that the ideas discussed here came as a spontaneous inspiration. They had their origin in long broodings. In this way we had been prepared for the situation which now confronted us; and although the alternatives originally envisaged were only vaguely held when the real position had cropped up it did not require much ingenuity or skill to give them concrete expression.

My purpose is to give a true picture of our actual position during these critical hours and the thoughts and hopes that tormented my mind as the one person responsible not only for the effective execution of the orders which I had received, but also the lives of the men and women entrusted to my authority. Beyond that I am personally completely indifferent to what the overcritical may think or say.

Chapter 9
Dublin Burning

There had been a noticeable slackening off in the firing against us on the forenoon of Wednesday, and during it a small reinforcement had come from the GPO direct to the Imperial Hotel. This group had in it a Captain Frank Thornton who arrived in full Volunteer uniform. Frank had been living in England and had returned to Ireland like many others in order to avoid the possibility of conscription into the British army. The majority of these were members of the Volunteer movement. They had been accommodated in a building in Kimmage and were somewhat humorously referred to as 'the refugees'. No braver or better body of Irishmen existed.

I had now two officers to assist me, Gerald Crofts having been provisionally promoted by myself to the rank of lieutenant. Thornton was, as I have said, already a captain of the Volunteers, a cheerful and alert soul ever-ready for any adventure and as such he was a tower of strength. Later he rose to the rank of colonel in the regular defence forces of the Free State, but, becoming involved in the somewhat absurd 'Tobin Mutiny' in 1924, his military career came to an end. This was a pity because Frank was capable of rising to the highest rank in that service. But it had its compensations in other activities, as he rose to a deserved eminence in our native insurance and industrial life. At the time I write of, he went under the assumed name of Frank Drennan as a further protection against seizure for military service on behalf of England.[86]

As a matter of record very many of these old 1916 comrades played a conspicuous part in the industrial life of the renewed Irish nation—Joe McGrath of the Hospitals Trust Ltd, Michael O'Reilly, Dr Seamus O'Ryan, Denis McCullagh, Sean MacEntee, Míceál Staines and very many others. They were a unique group of young men imbued with the ideal of Ireland once again a sovereign and completely free nation—'Gaelic from the centre to the sea'. They were rather unknown except to their intimates. If in subsequent years one could not always agree with their ideas and methods for attaining this noble ideal, one must not overlook the great spirit of bravery and self-sacrifice they displayed in the days of their youth.

And so Thursday dawned, a beautiful, clear spring day. It was well into noon before the unequal contest reached its full fury. The enemy had closed well up on the south side, slightly less so on the east and north. What was taking place on our west was beyond our ken. As far as one could judge by the firing there did not seem to be any link-up between the east and north lines of the British forces. True the Liffey and harbour intervened, but even so there appeared to be a lack of contact between these two points. I hoped it would continue so. Through this gap, if it continued to exist, lay our one hope of escaping to the open. That was the way, I was told, to Fairview.

As the volume of fire against us grew with the day, it was clear that heavy reinforcements had reached the enemy forces in the city. This suggested that our ring of occupied posts on the south and west had been either overcome or by-passed. To by-pass isolated points of occupation in a large city is by no means a difficult task and the fact that such had taken place revealed another weakness in Connolly's otherwise excellent plan of occupation and defence. In the enemy's objective of knocking out quickly the seat of the provisional government and general headquarters of the Irish Republican Army, by-passing was the obvious and least expensive means.

Our original plans for pinning down British forces *in situ*, so to speak, had failed, mainly through the confusion and doubt created by the cancellation order. Every passing hour spelt a still more slender hope of our breaking through. What might have been an easy manoeuvre on Tuesday night had become difficult by Wednesday night and might well be impossible on this Thursday night. But possible or impossible, we could not leave our assigned post until absolutely compelled to do so by raging, all-consuming fire.

All through that Thursday I kept as close a watch on the north-east side of our position as my continual rounds of the post permitted. Physically worn out, excitement alone kept me going. Fortunately I had the happy knack of catnapping at any time and whilst these rests were brief in the extreme they were nonetheless invaluable.

I simply have not words in which to convey my admiration of the men and women of my little garrison. Now ringed round completely with fire, expecting destruction at any moment from devastating weapons to which we had no effective reply, their spirits remained undaunted. Joking, laughter and even rough horseplay constantly echoed through the rooms. Every order was promptly obeyed, every reprimand was received in respectful and regretful silence. They had fought continually from Wednesday morning and their strict attention to orders had so far brought them all safely through the ordeal. The reverberant boom of shells, the ceaseless chatter of machine-guns, the vicious zip of snipers' bullets, these formed the horrid and incessant cacophony of the passing hours. And against it all was our rather pitiful crack, crack, crack of measured rifle fire.

We had no means of knowing whether we were inflicting any losses on the enemy. But we were certainly keeping his snipers on the move and even if that movement brought the enemy creeping ever-closer at least we were helping to keep it down to a crawl. There were no heroic dashes of assaulting troops, no attempts to carry positions by storming tactics, no inspiring and intoxicating blaring of bugles and trumpets. Only a creeping, insidious thing, like some foul disease ever-inexorably gnawing its way to the vital core.

The duel with the sniper in Trinity College had taken on an almost personal character. He was a rare shot and stuck at it with doggedness. He was a born soldier and up to every trick in the bag. After a burst of fire from us he would lie doggo; then the least visible movement on our part and a bullet from him would come whistling in. Occasionally I took a hand in the game, though it was wrong of me to do so, as it is the duty of the commander to command and not to engage unless in hand-to-hand fighting. But we could never get the old fox. That he had not inflicted heavy losses on us was due to the insistence that the men take proper advantage of all available cover when moving or firing.[87]

And so morning wore into noon, noon into evening, and evening into the gathering dusk of night. Fight, fight, fight.

Artillery was in action to the north of O'Connell Street as well as the south side of the quays. Shells were bursting all round. I could not understand why the artillery pieces had not been turned on us before this. We were now so many small posts pinned down and being compelled to fight to a finish or surrender. I felt convinced that the men, if they had a choice, would unhesitatingly have voted for a fight to the finish. But, come what may, it was plain to all on that Thursday that a very short time would decide the issue. We were fighting our last stand. The odds were at least sixty to one against us, but our greatest drawback was the lack of adequate arms. However, there would be no disgrace in a defeat under those circumstances.

Fires were blazing in Sackville Place and Lower Abbey Street, including Wynn's Hotel. Back from this area right on to the quays there appeared to be a whole series of fires. They were all the outcome of incendiary shells.

I stood on the rooftops in the gathering gloom. Dublin burning! What a sight! Gruesome, awe-inspiring. Man's inhumanity to man—there is nothing so brutal and callous in all creation. Columns of deep black, evil-looking smoke spiralled up into the darkening sky. Flames leaped, twisted, curled and danced fantastically and the glow of this inferno tinted every object with a lurid redness. The face of a Volunteer, as he looked towards me, took on this horrid tinge. It was as if all the evils that had tormented our people through the ages were now gathered in our metropolis and were having a witches' frenzy of ritual and grim stalking death. The scene etched itself deep on my memory never to be effaced except by death. It was a scene symbolic in its gruesomeness of the agony of the dear motherland through the long and tedious centuries of oppressive thraldom. Would it ever end?

The answer was a sniper's bullet, ricocheting off the chimney stack behind which I sheltered. I ducked instinctively and it went off screeching with impotent fury. Slowly, firing was slackening off. But the fires blazed on. Still the black smoke curled and shaped and dissolved in the blacker sky. Sparks flew upwards in cascades. Timbers crackled and burst with dull report. And yet, through it all one had a strange sense of appalling silence. That was the really strange part of one's feeling, a silence that was oppressive, palpable and even dismaying, an inarticulate sense of the presence of some evil spirit brooding and directing the whole scene like a master producer from behind the scenes.

I had only just descended when the long expected happened. An incendiary shell hit the premises of Messrs Hoyte, chemical and drug merchants. It was situated on the quay-side of our block of buildings. The minute the explosion occurred the order to evacuate was given. We could not fight any class of fire; and the fire we now faced would have taxed the capacity of several fire brigades, fully equipped.[88] There was no panic. My old guide appeared by my side. Quickly but methodically the men were got down from the roofs, as other men were moving from the rooms of the various premises through the holes in the walls towards Fagan's. In this work of marshalling the garrison both Thornton and Crofts rendered signal service. When we were finally all assembled in Fagan's we had a quick check-up to ensure that no one had been accidentally left behind. All were present and correct.

The last instruction given as the evacuation began was for everyone to bend low as they rushed across the street so that their heads would not be silhouetted above the line of the barricade. As it was, our side of the barricade was, fortunately, in shadow.

A section was sent across the street to break in the door on the opposite side. When this was done the garrison, including the four ladies, was sent across in quick rushes. This was quickly effected and during the whole of this flight across the street not a single angry shot was directed at us. This gave me great hope that the contemplated line of retreat was still open to us. If it were, then our chance of slipping through during the darkness and beginning a running fight in the rear of the enemy was reasonably good.

It was well for us, indeed, that we had discussed and to a small degree rehearsed this evacuation. The fire ate through the block of buildings, along its rear, with incredible speed. Perhaps the store of oils and chemicals in Hoyte's had given it an un-usual intensity. The last file of the garrison was only quitting the hallway when the fire came roaring into the kitchen of the premises. Had there been any delay or confusion the result might well have been horrible.

We had taken up the North Earl Street position on Monday night, had fought tremendous odds all through Wednesday and Thursday and had now evacuated without a single casualty. What fate awaited us in the byways of Dublin?

Chapter 10
The Attempted Breakthrough

As we quit our post in North Earl Street, the GPO was fighting bravely on. The tricolour was still waving atop of the great building, though to the rear great clouds of black smoke were swirling around it. It could only be a matter of hours until they, too, were forced to follow our example.

When all the garrison was safely ensconced in the building on the opposite side of the street, we made our way easily through the back door into a kind of covered passage. This led to a big doorway leading out into Cathedral Street, a short, very narrow street running from O'Connell Street to Marlborough Street.

Hope began to surge more fully. This was exactly the way I hoped to dribble through the now closely drawn British lines. If we could maintain this form of progress through back lanes, premises, old mews, and alleyways, we may not only get through but could do so with a minimum of loss.

Only a lurid light was reflected in the narrow street and we were drawn up on its shadow side. Forming the garrison into columns of fours—the easiest formation to handle in the circumstances—I divided it into an advance guard under myself, a main body under Crofts and a rear guard under Thornton.

I then ordered that we were to advance as silently as possible, no smoking or conversation. When we came to a crossing, the first file was to slip across as quickly and silently as possible, then wait for the arrival of the second file; the first was then to move off and the second to wait for the third, and so on until the whole body was safely across. This method would ensure that vital contact would not be lost and at the same time a steady advance would be maintained. It was carefully explained that if we ran into opposition the column would be formed up under the first and best available cover; that stock would then be taken of our position and the enemy's apparent distribution. We would endeavour to keep pushing on, but if this were found to be impossible then we would break into the best available building and make a last stand. Under no circumstances was anyone to fire a shot unless an order to do so was given. We were not to reveal ourselves to the enemy or let him gauge our strength. If he chose to think that we were a few scattered individuals trying to desert or escape, well, let him do so. All guns were then ordered to be loaded.

One problem remained. It was a difficult one. We could not bring with us our four gallant young ladies. We did not know what we were heading into, possibly an inferno of slaughter, and we certainly did not wish to land them in any such situation. But it was equally certain that they would not easily be persuaded to desert us. I asked Crofts if there was any place in the immediate locality where we could find sanctuary for them. He said that there was a presbytery just round the corner in Marlborough Street. Turning to the guide I asked him where we were going from here. He said we would turn up left through Marlborough Street and Crofts added that this would bring us

past the presbytery door. I then told Crofts to have two men
follow me up with the women in front of them when we came
to the presbytery, and when the door was opened not to stand
on ceremony but to rush them inside. I then called up the ladies
and with a final caution to make no noise, signalled the advance
to begin.

The whole of the locality through which we were passing was
lit up with a lurid glow from the raging fires. The roar and
crackle from the building we had just quitted was distinctly
audible. We learned afterwards that the garrison in the GPO
believed that we had been trapped by the extraordinary rapidity
with which the fire had eaten its way through the block of
buildings. As we had all bent double in crossing the street, the
barricade had concealed our passage from them. A section of
the post office garrison had then knelt down, and despite their
own desperate plight, had offered up a decade of the rosary for
us. It was typical of the grand spirit of comradeship which
pervaded all sections.

Arriving opposite the presbytery I signalled the column to
halt, and going up to the door rang the bell. The door was
opened almost at once by a priest. He asked only one question,
'Do you want sanctuary?'

'Not for ourselves, Father,' I replied, 'but for four young
ladies.'[89]

Whilst this very brief colloquy was proceeding the men had
seized the women, who struggled and resisted, and rushed them
up the short flight of steps and through the door. The moment
they were inside I pulled the door shut and signalled the
advance to continue. Pandemonium had broken out in the hall
of the presbytery. But the priest was evidently an understanding

and determined man, and to my great relief they did not succeed in rejoining us, as was evidently their intention judging from the row they kicked up. No doubt they were as determined to stick to their post and instructions as we were to ours. All honour to them. In a sense it was a scurvy trick I had played on them, but I had a great feeling of relief in succeeding so easily. Our respect for their courage and devotion would not permit us to drag them into some horrible situation.

As we advanced a short distance along Marlborough Street our guide took a quick turn to the right, down through what appeared to be a narrow and twisting laneway. Not a single shot or challenge had been, so far, directed towards us. We had every reason to continue to hope for the best of luck. Then, as we turned left out of this sheltered lane I found myself facing a wide, open and apparently long street. I at once signalled a halt.

Turning to the guide I asked him if he really meant to lead us down the length of this street. He replied yes, there was no other way, from where we stood, to Fairview. Others confirmed this.

Hurriedly I explained that this was the very type of street I wished most to avoid, that we would not get very far along such a thoroughfare. But the guide insisted that there was no other way to get to Fairview, adding that all the streets from this point ran parallel right down to the North Strand. If we could reach the Strand, he said, we would be all right. A hurried consultation with Thornton and Crofts and some of the Citizen Army men brought no better solution. All were of the opinion that if we could reach the North Strand—which was only a name to me—there would be plenty of hidden ways.[90]

I did not want to fight in the city any longer if I could possibly avoid it. There was nothing to be gained by it. What I wanted most ardently was to reach the enemy's rear, with plenty of manoeuvre area behind me. Then we could fight in earnest and possibly draw a lot of pressure off the GPO, which was most urgently needed. The enemy would be unaware of how many had broken through, at least for a time, and it was certain he would turn in some force to deal with us. But it would be open to us to refuse to be tied down and to keep on the move in a running fight.

So with a final word on the necessity of keeping contact, but with a heavy heart, I signalled the advance to continue.

The first crossing was negotiated without a hitch. But at the second crossing we were greeted with the command 'Halt' coming from our left and accompanied by a shot or two. Apparently the enemy was somewhat jumpy.

With a muttered 'Damn', we halted in the shelter of the block. The second section, despite increased firing, arrived safely. Rifle firing in the dark is an uncertain thing, but the annoying fact was that now the entire enemy force in the locality would be fully alerted. Much depended on how he held this section of streets. If it were held lightly we could still manage to get through, but if he were in any depth at all we were bunched. As far as I knew there had been no fighting in this obviously poor locality. But that was no sure index. I cautioned the second section not to move until the third and final one had arrived, and to pass the word back for a continued advance despite the firing.

As we were making the third crossing we were met with machine-gun and rifle fire, but no command to halt. Just as I reached the kerb on the opposite side I went down with a wound in the knee. Right behind me there was another thud.

Another man had been hit. Hastily crawling to the shelter of the block, whilst the other wounded man was being carried to the same haven, I prepared to take stock.

Despatching two men to scout the next crossing, I turned over to see the other casualty. I was told his name was Lemass.[91] He was very young and was certainly making light of his wound. He had a bad bullet wound right through the ankle. Fortunately it appeared to be clean but was bleeding profusely.

Gamely he tried to rise but collapsed with pain. Bandaging him as best we could, I put two more men to the task of gathering the rest of the garrison into our shelter as they arrived. We appeared to have reached journey's end. My own wound was comparatively slight, having been caused by a glancing bullet on the inside of the right knee. It was bleeding heavily and was very painful, but with a little help I could still manage to hobble.

The second section had by now arrived without mishap, despite the heavy fire to which they were subjected. The scouts came running back with word that they had met with heavy fire at the next crossing and that the fire in this case came from both sides. They also thought there was a barricade at the bottom of the long street. Visibility was none too good owing to the wreaths of smoke which were drifting through the air.

While they were reporting a man came running furiously along the centre of the street. We yelled at him to join us, but he seemed oblivious of our presence and continued his headlong pace. I feared panic had set in. As there was no sign of any more of the garrison arriving, I asked for volunteers to go back to try and make contact. Two men were selected and sent off on the hazardous journey. They returned safely, despite the firing, and reported that they had gone almost to Marlborough Street but could see no sign of the rest of the garrison. This was damnable. There were only nine in my group now, and two of us wounded. In view of the scouts' report it seemed useless to retrace our steps and try to join up with the main body. God alone knew where in the maze of streets they had gone aground, and to try to locate them with two wounded men could mean getting the whole nine wiped out to no purpose. We were in a hopeless position. We could offer no real resistance. The surprising thing was that the enemy was standing to his post and not attempting to send out investigating patrols.

I could move with a little help, but poor Lemass was clearly a stretcher case. Sending two men round the corner with instructions to hug the railings and break open the nearest doorway, I set the others to keep a close watch for any of our men that might appear, and to watch for any enemy attacking party.

The two men came back in a short time and reported that the hall door was wide open; it was a tenement house and the basement appeared to be empty. Detailing two men to remain on watch for stragglers, I had Lemass carried round the corner to the basement—the rest of the house appeared to be occupied by families. I sat down on the top step, ripped the leg of my trousers from the knee down and put on a bandage.

This basement room was poverty stricken in the extreme. A ramshackle bedstead stood in a corner facing the door at the bottom of the steps. There was practically no other furniture in the place. A coarse, lumpy mattress and a couple of terrible looking blankets were heaped on the bed. We settled Lemass as comfortably as possible on the bed, while he kept insisting that it was nothing and that he would be all right in a few minutes.

Sending two men out again along our former line of advance to try and make contact with the main body, I set about questioning the others as to our exact location.

No one seemed to know for certain. Opinions differed between Railway Street and Gloucester Street.[92] The difference may not have been much in actual distance, but even so, attempting to move forward without knowing exactly where we were might lead to real disaster. The old guide was positive it was Railway Street, but others were just as insistent that it wasn't. And they were all Dubliners. The only agreement was that we were facing in the general direction of Fairview. That was cold comfort. There was not much use, under the circumstances, trying to reach some ill-defined area if you did not know from where you were setting out. Furthermore, everybody was distinctly nervous because, they said, we were in the middle of a very hostile area, being full of 'dependants' allowances' women who would certainly betray us. Hearing this I had a sentry posted in the hall with instructions not to allow anyone out.

Everyone was agreed that we were still a long way from Fairview. The best I could hope for now was to get at least the bulk of my garrison together, hold another conference, try once more to discover where exactly we were, then search to see if there was any vacant building near at hand from which we could put up a last fight. No more than any of the others did I wish to remain a minute longer where we were. Apart from a hostile population, judging by sounds the building was crammed with women and children. To put up a fight here was clearly out of the question. In fact one of the inhabitants had made his appearance and asked us to leave on these very grounds.

After a considerable time the scouting party returned and reported they had searched back to Marlborough Street but could find no trace of the others anywhere. Many were of the opinion that the main body had gone back and joined up with the GPO garrison, but I was more inclined to the view that they had broken in somewhere in the locality. I expressed the hope that they were luckier than we were.[93] One point that was distinctly cheering was that all this scouting, despite the firing, resulted in no casualty. The fact that two were wounded was attributable more to ill-luck than accuracy of fire.

It was strange that the main body did not seem to detect our scouts. Possibly they had, but in the gloom and swirling smoke had mistaken them for enemy patrols. Before the evacuation the one thing I had forgotten was a series of short identification calls or signals to be used by us in the dark—and it was too late now. The only sensible thing was to lie doggo until day dawned so that we could locate our position with certainty, and try for a suitable nearby building to which we could retreat.

To have gone out in the dark and wandered around would have been sheer madness; and besides we could not abandon Lemass. Given a definite place to get to we might succeed in carrying him there, but we certainly could not carry him round in a series of aimless wanderings. There was nothing to be gained by keeping our sentries on the end of the cross street, so they were withdrawn. All hope of more of our men turning up had to be abandoned and if enemy patrols came along our present shelter would be discovered. Women were screaming and children bawling. It was a wonder the enemy had not come along to investigate the uproar.

It was a rotten situation. We were reduced to seven effectives with little ammunition and practically no food. Such reserves as we had in this line were back with the main body. If we were discovered we would have to quit the basement and move into an upper storey. If we tried to fight from there the enemy fire would be ruthless and the possible carnage amongst the women and children dreadful to think of.

We even considered turning all the inhabitants out to give us more freedom of action in case of need, but this was abandoned principally because it was too brutal. Besides, the noisy exodus would certainly attract the attention of the enemy. To wait for daylight seemed the only alternative and this was agreed on.

Physically I was washed out. My continual rounds of our post during Wednesday and Thursday, the lack of adequate sleep and the heavy responsibility of the attempted breakthrough had brought me to the verge of physical collapse. I simply would have to get some sleep if I were to carry on through the next day.

I posted the men, who were in little better shape than myself, in advantageous positions round the room, warning them to keep a sharp watch, not to talk or smoke, not to let me sleep more than an hour and to call me instantly if they had any suspicion of anything being wrong. I then drew my automatic, slipped off the safety catch, and rolled as best I could under the bed on which Lemass was groaning in pain that he made great efforts to suppress. The room was small and with eight men, the ninth being the sentry in the hall, under the bed was the only place available to me.

Oh, the fleas in that tenement! There must have been simply millions of them! They came joyously to the feast. They got under the bandage and at the wound. Had I not been so exhausted they would have driven me mad. As it was, I had no sooner stretched out than I was fast asleep and the fleas could have their undisturbed way with me.

Chapter 11
'Hands Up!'

I do not know how long I slept, but I awoke to fierce yelling and screamed orders to 'Hands up!' Raising my head, but still bemused with sleep, I saw the doorway crowded with British troops, some with grenades raised aloft and a young officer in front. Instinctively I took a pot shot at the officer. This brought me fully awake.

My men were standing in a close group in the centre of the room. They had evidently been taken by complete surprise. Rolling out from under the bed and standing up behind them, I whispered to them to put up their hands. There was no other course possible. We were lucky beyond imagination. Why the troops did not fling a grenade when I fired is a complete mystery to me to this day, as the troops were themselves in a state of panic, their young officer the worse of the lot. Had they flung a grenade, owing to the confined nature of the wretched basement, the carnage would have been complete and they themselves would have suffered considerably.

The young lieutenant kept shouting at the top of his voice: 'Who fired that shot?' It was rather a foolish question as well as an unreasonable one. But no one in our group made any answer. We just stood there, mute, with our hands raised up in response to the imperative command. A sergeant, obviously an old soldier, rushed into the room and got behind us—an unnecessary movement as there was no exit door from this room. The officer followed him still yelling to know who fired the shot. It was evident that whoever fired the shot, if revealed, would receive short shrift. In the end one of my men said that no one had fired a shot, and if one had been fired it must have been one of the soldiers. This naïve evasion made the young officer hopping mad. He declared if we did not tell him who fired the shot he would have us all shot, and he held up his arm to show us a bullet hole through his sleeve.

The same man continued to argue that none of us had fired a shot as none of us had weapons near at hand with which to do so. The men had left their rifles where I had posted them and had gradually drawn nearer to each other in the centre of the room as they engaged in whispered conversations and arguments about our position. The sentry on the door had retreated on the approach of the troops. Why they did not waken me when he came down from the hall I do not know, possibly they were too deeply involved in their arguments to pay much heed to him. And as I rolled from under the bed I had dropped my automatic behind a pile of rags. So there was a semblance of substance in the man's argument.

At any rate the sergeant finally came to the rescue by saying that they had better get outside and see if there were any more of us in the locality. We were then prodded upstairs with bayonets, but the prods, I am bound to record, were without venom. Poor Lemass was dragged somewhat roughly from the bed, but our comrades came to both our assistance and helped us up the short flight of stairs. Personally I felt very humiliated at being caught napping in this way, but reflecting on it afterwards I felt it was inevitable under the circumstances, and, all things considered, rather fortunate. The majority of the inhabitants of the tenement had congregated on the first landing and showered curses upon us as we appeared. Several of the women called on the soldiers to shoot the '— Sinn Féiners'.

Outside in the street the officer again started his demand to know who fired the shot and again exhibited his uniform sleeve. It was difficult to imagine which concerned him most, his lucky escape from death or his damaged tunic. However, we all remained mute. In the hustling upstairs I had managed to whisper to the men to refrain from making remarks. In face of our stubborn silence he ordered the sergeant to search us, possibly hoping by that means to identify a leader. Bless that old sergeant! He did a thorough job of searching. He pulled everything indiscriminately out of our pockets—money, watches, wallets, letters, etc.—and without a single glance at them flung them in a common heap on the ground. It would be impossible to tell who owned any particular object unless the owner chose to do so. The officer during this process kept striding angrily up and down. As the sergeant kept on vigorously carrying out his order he muttered under his breath: 'The young so-and-so is off his head.' The search over, the sergeant saluted and reported: 'No weapons, Sir.'

After a momentary pause, the lieutenant ordered us to march across the street to be lined up in single file and shot. On this command a cheer went up from the women who had now congregated round the doorway and I verily believe they would have cheered louder still if they saw us fall dead in front of their eyes. Just as we were about to cross the street on what we believed was our last journey a captain turned the corner. On his appearance we were halted. Had we, in fact, been lined up on the opposite side, I would have confessed to being the one who fired the shot. It was the least I could have done. It would have been utterly irresponsible to have stood there and have my comrades shot down for what was my own individual act; at the same time I had no intention of revealing myself until the very last moment. With the exception of the sergeant the soldiers were all on the young side and, whatever their individual opinions might be, I had no doubt that they would carry out their orders with that almost bovine indifference which discipline instils into the common soldier. To them it would be all part of the day's work.

The captain had come strolling round the corner of the block in the most casual manner imaginable. Casualness, indeed, seemed to be his outstanding characteristic. We stood mutely awaiting his pleasure. The lieutenant began an excited statement of what had happened, dramatically exhibiting again his tunic sleeve by way of more vivid illustration, and ended up by saying he was going to shoot us. The captain listened to the tale with the same air of casual indifference, and when the lieutenant finished he turned to the sergeant and said: 'March the prisoners to the Custom House, sergeant.'

Seeing that two of us were wounded, the captain ordered some of the soldiers to sling their rifles and assist us. As we moved off down the street the sergeant muttered: 'You're a lucky lot of so-and-so's.' We could not have agreed more. My pocketful of despatches, reports and orders, was left lying in an ownerless heap in the street, which was lucky for me.

Some of the Dublin men found out afterwards that, just before dawn, a young woman had got out through a back window, made her way to the enemy and betrayed us. Generations of these people had, through economic necessity, gone into the British army. They knew no loyalty but to their bread and butter, or what there was of it. And they hated Sinn Féiners as the ones who were likely to deprive them of that same bread and butter. But however all that may be, we had come luckily out of a very grim situation. So far as we were concerned the Rising was at an end. We had been spared to fight another day. But what of our comrades? Were they fighting for life and liberty, or dead, or prisoners like ourselves?

Arriving at the Custom House we were shoved into what appeared to be a light and air shaft in the centre of a great block of buildings. It was rather small, paved with large flags and entered by two opposite archways. It was a passageway as well as a light and air shaft. Two armed and silent sentries took up their stand in each archway.

As the morning wore on we were joined by most of our lost comrades, who were brought in in small batches. They had lost contact during the intensity of the firing directed against them and the semi-gloom; had become hopelessly scattered; and had made the best shelter they could. Like ourselves they had hoped to establish contact again when day dawned.

There did not appear to have been any losses so far and we hoped that those who were still unaccounted for were also safe. It turned out later that Harry Manning, one of our crack shots on the roofs, had received about fourteen bullet wounds and a young man named Flannigan, son of an RIC man, had also been badly wounded.[94] Otherwise everyone had escaped unscathed, except the young man who had elected to try and make his way to the GPO garrison and whom I was never able afterwards to trace.

About eleven o'clock in the morning we were brought up in small batches to an orderly room before a colonel of the Queen's Regiment. Our names, addresses and occupations were taken down and we were subjected to a severe questioning. The colonel was very austere, very hostile, but he did his job with meticulous care. I gave only half my name—James Brennan—and gave my occupation as journalist. On hearing this the colonel ordered me to be again searched. I was stripped almost to the bare nuff. He evidently did not like journalists. Asked what I was doing in Dublin, I replied that I had come up for the races, had got caught up in the Rising and had been wounded. He stared at me very hard for a moment and then ordered my removal. He did not believe a word of what I had said, which was a discreet mixture of lies and truth. Had my despatches been discovered as belonging to me I would have been quickly segregated and my ultimate fate would have been very different. Bless that old sergeant. At this preliminary questioning the British military were not assisted by the political section of the Dublin Metropolitan Police. It would not have made any difference in my case if they had been, for I was confident that I was unknown to them. My real object in suppressing part of my name was to prevent the local RIC in Wexford getting to know of my whereabouts quickly. They would certainly have taken more than a casual interest in my activities. I attribute my escape from a court martial to this suppression.

From the time we were arrested one question was asked of us by all and sundry—even our old friend the sergeant asked it on the way to the Custom House—'Where are the German snipers?' It amounted almost to an obsession. No amount of denial seemed to have any effect. The fire from our snipers with the German Mauser rifles had been so accurate and, apparently, had inflicted so many casualties that nothing would convince our captors but that we had professional German snipers cunningly hidden away. We drew a certain amount of comfort out of the question. It brought home to us that our efforts on behalf of our country had not been so futile as might seem on a casual glance.

When this ordeal was over and we were again lying down quietly on the flags, I whispered that no matter what abuse was hurled at us no notice of it was to be taken. Nothing would be gained in our situation by becoming involved in political arguments.

It is only fair to say that once we got clear of our overexcited captor, the British officers and troops treated us with all the kindness and consideration their own position permitted. One officer went so far as to apologise for the fact that no food had been offered to us. He explained that they had no food even for themselves, and that practically all their men had been on duty continuously for hours and hours without relief or food. In view of this I can only say that their control of their tempers was remarkable.

There was a tremendous craze amongst the officers for souvenirs. Poor Frank Thornton, who was in full Volunteer uniform, was practically denuded of tunic buttons. They were not just taken by the officers but courteously asked for, and he gave them up with typical good humour. Being in uniform he was taken for the officer in charge of the group, and no one, least of all Frank himself, sought to enlighten our captors.

Despite the cold hard flags of our quarters most of us slept through the late forenoon and early afternoon. It was a sleep

induced by both physical exhaustion and hunger. In the evening
we chatted with those of the garrison who visited us from time
to time. They were coming to have a close look at those queer
animals, the 'wild Irish'. In between we sang patriotic songs.
Gerald Crofts had a glorious voice and was always ready with a
song whenever called on. He was a wonderful character, always
thinking of the comfort of others and ready to do anything to
oblige. He gave a great fillip to our morale.

Some time in the evening, when a small group of off-duty
troops had gathered at one of the archways and were indulging
in some sarcastic remarks, a captain came in through the
opposite archway. He had in his hand one of our arms
contribution cards and began to question Frank Thornton
about them. Frank explained that the men had contributed
what they could each week out of their meagre wages to a fund
to buy arms with which to try and free our country and that the
card constituted a receipt. The look of astonishment on the
officer's face made us all laugh. 'Do you seriously mean to tell
me that you men have been saving out of your wages in order to
buy rifles to fight for your country?'

When he was told that he held the proof in his hand he asked:

'Did not your leaders get all the money they needed from
Germany?'

'They certainly did not', Frank replied with some heat. 'Any
German rifles we have been using have been paid for with our
own money. We certainly wanted rifles from anywhere we could
get them, but we wanted no money from Germany or any other
country.'

'No one could ever understand this damned country!', exclaimed the officer.

As he came in to us he must have overheard some of the remarks of his troops which, truth to say, were harmless enough. He read them a lesson on patriotism, which sounded strange coming from a man who had just confessed he could not understand the action of patriots, and actually went so far as to hold us up as examples to his own men. He finished by declaring he would have our quarters put out of bounds for all off-duty troops. When the troops had left he began showering praise upon us, and wound up an interesting interview by stating that we would be great fighters if only we had the khaki on. To which we good-humouredly replied that he certainly did not understand the Irish.

I suppose that the real trouble with the English generally is that inherent belief in their own rectitude which leads them to believe that whatever they think or say or do is the last word in righteousness: a feeling that they are God's own chosen people, with a signal destiny to own the earth and to bring enlightenment to all peoples. It is a sentiment which can be traced back to Calvinism and forms the basis of all jingoism.[95] Except for this irritating characteristic the English, by and large, are not a bad people. The trouble lies with their politicians and statesmen who seem always to suffer from an overdose of this characteristic, incapable of understanding anything beyond its orbit.

Chapter 12
The Aussie Sergeant

All this time we had been lounging around as best we could in our cramped quarters. We were unwashed, unshaven and unkempt, and must have looked disreputable in the extreme. I had not received or asked for any medical assistance, nor indeed did I require any. My wound was slight, more a glancing wound from a fragment than a direct hit from a bullet which would have shattered the knee completely. It was extremely painful and had bled a lot, but I had managed to keep it clean and renew the bandage from time to time. The fact that my right trouser leg had been completely slit from just above the knee gave me a somewhat scarecrow appearance.

Towards midnight when we had been left in peace for some time, had finished saying the rosary, and were trying to settle down as best we could for a night's rest on the hard flags, the figure of a sergeant in the uniform of the Australian forces made its appearance in one of the archways. He began straight away to shower abuse upon us. He was particularly vile in his language at times, and keeping our tempers was no easy matter. What made it so difficult for us to bear was that his language was in such violent contrast to what we had hitherto met with, but we all lay quiet and ignored him. Besides which he was slightly drunk, and belonging to the Australian forces he was more on a sightseeing tour than on duty. That we lay so quiet and said nothing was by no means an indication that we were broken in spirit. There was nothing to be gained by entering into a violent argument with a slightly intoxicated NCO.

He ended his tirade by demanding to know where were 'the — German snipers?' This, too, we ignored. Then quite suddenly and without any apparent cause, he took an absolutely different course and began to shower praise upon us. This was so extraordinary that most of us sat up to listen to him. We wondered if he sensed that a British officer might be in the offing. He continued to assert that we were great fighters, 'considering'. He again enquired about the German snipers.

The man began to intrigue me. His uncalled for abuse, then his sudden change of tune, all set me wondering what was at the back of it. At first we had thought that he was merely drunk or that a pal had been killed—this puts many an otherwise steady soldier off balance. With what patience I could muster I began to explain to him, as we had dozens of times previously, that we had no German snipers of any sort with us. It was on the tip of my tongue to tell him to go up north and he might find a few German snipers amongst the Orangemen. We were getting a bit peeved over this matter.

But he broke in impetuously to say that if that were so, some of us were wonderful shots. This showed that he was not so drunk after all and I looked at him for a moment, wishing that the light was better. I decided to try him out with a bit of praise.

'There were some pretty good snipers amongst yourselves', I said.

He asked me what made me say that and in reply I told him the incident of our cable with the canister attached to it. The moment he grasped what I was saying he gave an exultant war-whoop and exclaimed: 'Did I get it?'

The reply rather staggered me for a moment. The thought that this was the individual with whom we had had the long duel came as a bit of a shock. He came in and sat down beside me. There seemed no doubting his sheer delight, and it was apparent that he had been on a personal prowl seeking out those with whom he had had the duel.

'Not quite', I replied when he had settled himself down beside me. 'But you went within less than half an inch of completely messing up our only line of communication with the GPO.' Then looking at him very hard I queried: 'Are you the so-and-so that was sniping at us out of the corner of Trinity College?'

All were now sitting up listening avidly to the conversation. The two sentries, nearly as physically exhausted as ourselves, were half asleep at their posts and took no apparent interest at what was being said.

With obvious delight he admitted he was the sniper in question. He said he was sure he had got it, as he only saw it the once when he had shot at it. I explained that the canister was a mistake and when he holed it so near the twine, we did not use it anymore. Lowering his voice he began to talk about the two-day duel. His delight increased when he learned that I had taken a hand in it several times. I told him I could not understand how it was that I had missed him so often as I was considered to be a first class shot with a rifle. He smiled tolerantly and bragged that his speciality was snap shooting. There was not a trace of rancour in his voice or manner towards us. It seemed as if he looked upon the deadly duel as a great game in which he had personally triumphed, and I verily believe that even if he had been severely wounded he would not have borne any malice. It was a most extraordinary contrast to his initial abuse. He led us to believe that we had caused a lot of casualties among the partially trained troops sent against us. After swapping yarns of this sort for some time he arose and, saying that he would be back shortly, he left. I remember Thornton saying, after he had gone, that the man must be crazy.

He came back to us in a short time with a Jacob's biscuit tin in one hand and a mug of cold tea in the other. Apologising that that was all he could scrounge, he handed the mug of tea to myself saying it was for 'Auld Lang Syne'. He asked that the biscuits be eaten up and that we not say anything about where we got them. He then left for good.[96]

The biscuit tin was a little less than a quarter full of broken biscuits which we shared around. I thought the cold tea was the most delicious I had ever drunk. None of the men would take any of the tea from me knowing that I was unusually thirsty from my slight wound. It was a weird interlude and provided us with much food for thought.

The really bad news reached us shortly afterwards. That it was expected did not detract from its ominousness. Our friend, the captain of the contribution card, came in to inform us of the unconditional surrender by general headquarters. Some of the men refused to believe it and others became depressed. For myself it was no more than I had expected. What else could be expected? We were fighting in our own country and for our own country: the people and property of the metropolis of that country had to be considered. Once the enemy had succeeded in drawing his cordon close around us, and was using shell fire indiscriminately, there was nothing else that could have been done.

Had there been a concerted effort to break out to the open country whilst there was still time, a running fight for some weeks—perhaps months—could have been kept up, a protracted struggle that would have seriously embarrassed Anglo-American relations and have made a mockery of Britain's claim to be fighting for the freedom of small nations.

As things were, the members of the provisional government had acted for the best and in the national interest. The blood sacrifice had been made; the heritage of resistance had been maintained; the national honour had been redeemed from the slime of constitutionalism. Nothing more could be done under the circumstances except bind up our wounds and await our time. The greatest loss, materially speaking, was the wholesale loss of arms involved in unconditional surrender. But that too could, in time, be remedied by resolute men.

There was no mistaking the jubilation with which the British received the news. Officers and men alike went about with very pleased smiles on their faces, as if a great load had been removed from their shoulders. The impression was left on one's mind that most of them had no great heart in the duty they felt they had to perform.

It was greatly to their credit that neither officers nor men made any attempt to mock us with the fact that it was an unconditional surrender. Indeed there was a complete absence of personal hostility and a disposition to fraternise, mixed with an understandable curiosity.

Nor could there be any doubting the fact that the military were disturbed by the situation in the country. What that situation was we ourselves did not know. We had heard a little about the masterly action at Ashbourne under Thomas Ashe and Richard Mulcahy. But the military knew that Wexford and Galway were out, showing that Eoin MacNeill's cancellation order was not one hundred per cent effective; and they knew that news of the stiff fighting in Dublin had reached the country corps despite the breakdown in transport and communications. Any moment the flame of revolt might spread over the country. The problem for the British then would take on a totally different complexion.

The hard, inescapable fact was that the 'Sinn Féin rebellion'—as the British and *The Irish Times* loved to call it—was over. But where people are enslaved hope must never be abandoned.

Chapter 13
In Richmond Barracks

In due course we were moved from the Custom House to Richmond Barracks. There were but little demonstrations of hostility directed towards us. Along the route the few people that were congregated looked on rather apathetically as if they had not got over the shock of the week's hectic events. We kept up the best front we could, and frequently broke into patriotic songs of which Crofts was the moving spirit. Our attitude was not one of defiance; we simply wanted the people who watched us go by to know that we were by no means downhearted and that we in no way regretted the action we had taken.

At this time, the 18th Royal Irish Regiment was in occupation of Richmond Barracks. To my great surprise, we were not segregated and isolated. The members of the garrison were allowed to mix freely with us in the barrack room in which we were temporarily housed. We were not the only insurgent prisoners confined in this great military barrack and many of my men recognised and had a great powwow with city friends and acquaintances.

I would have felt very much out of it and alone but that the Royal Irish was the territorial unit for County Wexford: I knew many of the soldiers and they knew me. We were received and treated with the greatest kindness by the NCOs and men of the 18th. I do not know personally if the statement in the second proclamation of the provisional government to the citizens of Dublin that Irish regiments in the British army had refused to act against their fellow-countrymen was founded on fact or mere rumour. What I do know is this. Many of the NCOs and men of the 18th Regiment were very dissatisfied that we had not given them a chance to join us. Practically all those whom I knew personally, and some I didn't know, came and unhesitatingly voiced that sentiment to me.

When I pointed out that there was nothing to prevent them seizing their barracks and sending us word to that effect, and that we would have given them every welcome, they replied that they had considered that plan several times but lacked any assurance that their help would be accepted. If it were not, then they would have been in the devil's own pickle. They would have mutinied to no one's advantage, and would be shot to pieces.

I queried why they had not sought to contact the Volunteers privately beforehand and thus find out whether their services would be welcome or not. They replied that they did not take all this volunteering and drilling seriously, that in fact they never once thought it would lead to a rebellion.

Oh, how often had I listened to that excuse all through Monday night and all day on Tuesday! In view of the antics of the Irish Parliamentary Party and their 'National' Volunteers—most of whom had joined the British army—it was a reasonable point of view. But the number of nationally minded people in Ireland who did not take the Irish Volunteer movement seriously must have been extraordinarily high.

One clear impression left on my mind by these muttered confidences was that the 18th were boiling mad that they had not had a hand in the fighting. As several of them said, they had plenty of arms (of which we were pitifully short) and they would have made a tremendous difference to the quality of the fighting. And possibly to the final result. Had we made any attempt to invest their barracks, they would have seized the barracks at once and joined us. Such is the unpredictable nature of these adventures in the realm of patriotism.[97]

It must be pointed out, too, that all the soldiers in this regiment were not Wexford men, nor indeed Irishmen; there was a sprinkling of English, Scotch and Welsh. Neither were all the officers Wexford men. A number of them were, indeed, members of county families, but other nationalities were represented also. This added to the problem of the nationally minded members.

At any rate, they fed us well and lent us shaving and toilet kits. For the first time in days I enjoyed the luxury of a shave and wash. In fact the troops were overanxious to do us every little kindness they could anticipate.

As we were sitting on the edge of cots chatting with the troops the door opened and a small group of British officers came in. We all came to attention. What brought us up so quickly was the fact that Comdt General Joseph Mary Plunkett, our chief of staff, was in their midst.

How terrible he looked! His throat was still heavily bandaged, with the tunic opened below the second button. He had no hat on and a brown army blanket was draped across his stooped shoulders. He looked weary and on the verge of collapse from exhaustion. As he crossed the threshold he paused, and I crossed the room impulsively to him, saluted and held out my hand. He took it in a gentle clasp and to my query as to how he was, he replied that he was not too bad. The officers with him were treating him with every courtesy and made no demur against my intrusion. With a slight wave of his hand and a low-voiced 'God bless you all', this utterly unselfish young patriot passed on with his escort. Just days later he was married to Grace Gifford only a few hours before he was taken out and shot to death.

The British have a passion for compiling nominal rolls. To the uninitiated it all seems needlessly repetitious and a senseless waste of time. It was however a routine necessary for instilling, or helping to instil, that iron discipline which was so characteristic of the older British army. Anyhow, it was not long before a colour-sergeant, accompanied by a junior officer, came in and started writing up our names, addresses and occupations. In view of the fact that so many of the troops knew me I saw no point in again giving the name, James Brennan; neither did I see any point in giving my full name which is long and cumbersome. And in view of the hostility of the colonel of the Queen's Regiment to journalists I saw no point in again giving that as my occupation. At that time I was a freelance writer and not the professional journalist I later became. So I gave my occupation as that of a farmer, which was true enough.[98]

But it was not to pass off as simply as that. They had the nominal rolls from where we had been held previously. Asked why I had given a different name and occupation, I indignantly denied doing so and sought to throw the blame on the colonel in the Custom House. As prisoners were still pouring in they were not inclined to be pernickety. So long as they did not suspect you of being a 'leader', they did not bother you very much; but if they once got suspicious that you were somebody other than you appeared to be you were promptly segregated and in for a hell of a time of questioning.

We were frequently marched over to the barrack gymnasium and lined up for inspection by members of the detective branch. The purpose of these inspections was to pick out and drag forth for trial by court martial anyone who had been prominent in the Sinn Féin and Volunteer movements.

On one such occasion I was standing beside Gerald Crofts. When he saw the detective for whom we were lined up he whispered to me:

'We are all right this time. He is a friend of our family and a very decent man.'

Slowly the sleuth came down along the line, closely scrutinising each prisoner. None of these inspections held any terrors for me as I was an unknown quantity to the Dublin detectives. There was no pause in the present inspection until he came opposite Crofts. Here he stopped.

'Oh, Gerald, how did you get here?', challenged the sleuth. 'Step forward, please.'

The 'friend of the family' had picked out Gerald for trial by court martial. He was sentenced to ten years' penal servitude (five years remitted). Poor Frank Thornton being in the uniform of a captain in the Volunteers was picked out early and sentenced to twenty years' penal servitude (ten years remitted).[99]

During our time in Richmond Barracks rumours flew thick and fast around us. Whence they arose no one knew, but they were certainly persistent. We were all going to be shot in groups; great common graves were being dug in all the barracks in Dublin. And so on. We were now in such a mood that we did not care very much what happened to us. We did not exactly want to die but if we had to it would not worry us very much. We had all expected to meet death in the course of the fighting.

So death had no real terror for us. We were becoming restless, moody and devil-may-carish. We knew that the courts martial were working overtime; and we knew of the execution of the leaders.

However, these ugly rumours were finally laid when it became known that on 30 April no less than two hundred prisoners were evacuated from Richmond Barracks for internment in Knutsford Jail, England. On 3 May, a further three hundred and eight prisoners—of whom I was one—were evacuated from Richmond Barracks for internment in Knutsford Jail.[100]

As we tramped and hobbled down the quays, under heavy escort, we were pelted by garbage and filthy epithets by the scum of the city. Doubtless, we presented a sorry spectacle to have so impudently challenged the might of the British empire. We had tried and lost, and for us it appeared *vae victis!*

But how little we ourselves realised, much less those who looked on at our bedraggled passing, that within two years we would sweep the Irish Parliamentary Party and constitutionalism out of the country for ever and a day; that we would set up in Dublin a native parliament known as Dáil Éireann; that we would renew the fight with strategy and tactics better calculated to even the imbalance between ourselves and our ancient enemy; that within the short period of five years from the quelling of our Rising we would compel a British prime minister to ask for a truce to the fighting from a handful of untrained and only partially armed Irish patriots! Yet these were the mighty developments that lay in the womb of time.

We triumphed in our failure because we were the party of self-sacrifice and tradition; we were the party that stood loyally by the historical conception of the sovereignty of the Irish nation. The blood of our martyred dead had transfused new life into our people. We were no longer a minority battling against overwhelming odds: sacrifice had turned the scales.

Documents of the Rising

The first insurgent proclamation was in the form of a large poster and was undated. See pp. 44–5 and 50 for further treatment of the proclamation.[101]

POBLACHT NA hEIREANN

THE PROVISIONAL GOVERNMENT

OF THE

IRISH REPUBLIC

TO THE PEOPLE OF IRELAND.

IRISHMEN AND IRISHWOMEN: In the name of God and of the dead generations from which she receives her old tradition of nationhood, Ireland, through us, summons her children to her flag and strikes for her freedom.

Having organised and trained her manhood through her secret revolutionary organisation, the Irish Republican Brotherhood, and through her open military organisations, the Irish Volunteers and the Irish Citizen Army, having patiently perfected her discipline, having resolutely waited for the right moment to reveal itself, she now seizes that moment, and, supported by her exiled children in America and by gallant allies in Europe, but relying in the first on her own strength, she strikes in full confidence of victory.

We declare the right of the people of Ireland to the ownership of Ireland, and to the unfettered control of Irish destinies, to be sovereign and indefeasible. The long usurpation of that right by a foreign people and government has not extinguished the right, nor can it ever be extinguished except by the destruction of the Irish people. In every generation the Irish people have asserted their right to national freedom and sovereignty; six times during the past three hundred years they have asserted it in arms. Standing on that fundamental right and again asserting it in arms in the face of the world, we hereby proclaim the Irish Republic as a Sovereign Independent State, and we pledge our lives and the lives of our comrades-in-arms to the cause of its freedom, of its welfare, and of its exaltation among the nations.

The Irish Republic is entitled to, and hereby claims, the allegiance of every Irishman and Irishwoman. The Republic guarantees religious and civil liberty, equal rights and equal opportunities to all its citizens, and declares its resolve to pursue the happiness and prosperity of the whole nation and of all its parts, cherishing all the children of the nation equally, and oblivious of the differences carefully fostered by an alien government, which have divided a minority from the majority in the past.

Until our arms have brought the opportune moment for the establishment of a permanent National Government, representative of the whole people of Ireland and elected by the suffrages of all her men and women, the Provisional Government, hereby constituted, will administer the civil and military affairs of the Republic in trust for the people.

We place the cause of the Irish Republic under the protection of the Most High God, Whose blessing we invoke upon our arms, and we pray that no one who serves that cause will dishonour it by cowardice, inhumanity or rapine. In this supreme hour the Irish nation must, by its valour and discipline and by the readiness of its children to sacrifice themselves for the common good, prove itself worthy of the august destiny to which it is called.

Signed on Behalf of the Provisional Government,

THOMAS J. CLARKE,

SEAN Mac DIARMADA,	THOMAS MacDONAGH,
P. H. PEARSE,	EAMONN CEANNT,
JAMES CONNOLLY,	JOSEPH PLUNKETT.

———

The second proclamation issued was also in the form of a poster and undated.

THE PROVISIONAL GOVERNMENT
to the
CITIZENS OF DUBLIN
The Provisional Government of the Irish Republic salutes
the Citizens of Dublin on the momentous occasion of
the proclamation of a
SOVEREIGN INDEPENDENT IRISH STATE
now in course of being established by Irishmen in Arms.

The Republican forces hold the lines taken up at Twelve noon on Easter Monday, and nowhere, despite fierce and almost continuous attack of the British troops, have the lines been broken through. The country is rising in answer to Dublin's call, and the final achievement of Ireland's freedom is now, with God's help, only a matter of days. The valour, self-sacrifice, and discipline of Irish men and women are about to win for our country a glorious place among the nations.

Ireland's honour has already been redeemed: it remains to vindicate her wisdom and her self-control.

All citizens of Dublin who believe in the right of their Country to be free will give their allegiance and their loyal help to the Irish Republic. There is work for everyone: for the men in the fighting line, and for the women in the provision of food and first aid. Every Irishman and Irishwoman worthy of the name will come forward to help their common country in this her supreme hour.

Able bodied Citizens can help by building barricades in the streets to oppose the advance of the British troops. The British troops have been firing on our women and on our Red Cross. On the other hand, Irish Regiments in the British Army have refused to act against their fellow countrymen.

The Provisional Government hopes that its supporters—which means the vast bulk of the people of Dublin—will preserve order and self-restraint. Such looting as has already occurred has been done by hangers-on of the British Army. Ireland must keep her new honour unsmirched.

We have lived to see an Irish Republic proclaimed. May we live to establish it firmly, and may our children and our children's children enjoy the happiness and prosperity which freedom will bring.

Signed on behalf of the Provisional Government,

P. H. Pearse,

Commanding in Chief the Forces of the Irish Republic and President of the Provisional Government.

―――

On the second day of the Rising general headquarters issued a four-page newspaper measuring ten inches by seven and a half inches.

Irish War News

The Irish Republic

Vol. 1, No. 1, Dublin, Tuesday April 25th, 1916.

Price One Penny.

Stop Press!

The Irish Republic.

[Irish] War News is published today because a momentous thing has happened. The Irish Republic has been proclaimed in Dublin, and a Provisional Government has been appointed to administer its affairs.

The following has been named as the Provisional Government:

Thomas J. Clarke,

Sean Mac Diarmada,

P. H. Pearse,

James Connolly,

Thomas MacDonagh,

Eamon Ceannt,

Joseph Plunkett.

The Irish Republic was proclaimed by poster which was prominently displayed in Dublin.

At 9.30 a.m. this morning the following statement was made by Commandant-General P. H. Pearse:

The Irish Republic was proclaimed in Dublin on Easter Monday, April 24, at 12 noon. Simultaneously with the issue of the proclamation of the Provisional Government the Dublin Division of the Army of the Republic, including the Irish Volunteers, the Citizen Army, Hibernian Rifles, and other bodies occupied dominating positions in the city. The G.P.O. was seized at 12 noon, the Castle attacked at the same moment, and shortly afterwards the Four Courts were occupied. The Irish troops hold the City Hall and dominate the Castle. Attacks were immediately commenced by the British forces, and everywhere were repulsed. At the moment of writing this report (9.30 a.m., Tuesday) the Republican forces hold their positions and the British forces have nowhere broken through. There has been heavy and continuous fighting for nearly 24 hours, the casualties of the enemy have been much more numerous than those on the Republican side. The Republican forces every-where are fighting with splendid gallantry. The populace of Dublin are plainly with the Republic, and the officers and men are everywhere cheered as they march through the city. The whole centre of the city is in the hands of the Republic, whose flag flies from the G.P.O.

Commandant-General P. H. Pearse is Commandant in Chief of the Army of the Republic and is President of the Provisional Government. Commandant-General James Connolly is commanding Dublin districts.

Communication with the country is largely cut, but reports to hand show that the country is rising. Bodies of men from Kildare and Fingal have already been reported in Dublin.

————

Copy of order issued by Commandant General James Connolly

Army of the Irish Republic
(Dublin Command)
Date, 25th April, 1916.

Headquarters,

To the Officer in charge, Reis and D.B.C.[102]

The main purpose of your post is to protect our wireless station. Its secondary purpose is to observe Lower Abbey Street and Lower O'Connell Street. Commandeer in the D.B.C. whatever food and utensils you require. Make sure of a plentiful supply of water wherever your men are. Break all glass in windows of the room occupied by you for fighting purposes. Establish a connection between your forces in the D.B.C. and in Reis building. Be sure that the stairways leading immediately to your rooms are well barricaded. We have a post in the house at the corner of Bachelor's Walk, in the Hotel Metropole, in the Imperial Hotel, in the General Post Office. The directions from which you are likely to be attacked are from the Custom House, or from the far side of the river, D'Olier Street, or Westmoreland Street. We believe there is a sniper in McBirney's on the far side of the river.

James Connolly,

Commandant-General.

——

Copy of order found on the body of The O'Rahilly, who was shot dead while fighting in Henry Place.

Army of the Irish Republic
(Dublin Command)
Headquarters, April 28, 1916.

To the Soldiers.

This is the fifth day of the establishment of the Irish Republic, and the flag of our country still floats from the most important buildings in Dublin, and is gallantly protected by the officers and Irish soldiers in arms throughout the country. Not a day passes without seeing fresh postings of Irish soldiers eager to do battle for the old cause. Despite the utmost vigilance of the enemy we have been able to get in information telling us how the manhood of Ireland, inspired by our splendid action, are gathering to offer up their lives if necessary in the same holy cause. We are hemmed in because the enemy feels that in this building is to be found the heart and inspiration of our great movement.

Let us remind you what you have done. For the first time in 700 years the flag of a free Ireland floats triumphantly in Dublin City.

The British Army, whose exploits we are forever having dinned into our ears, which boasts of having stormed the Dardanelles and the German lines on the Marne, behind their artillery and machine guns are afraid to advance to the attack or storm any position held by our forces. The slaughter they suffered in the first few days has totally unnerved them and they dare not attempt again an infantry attack on our positions.

Our Commandants around us are holding their own.

Commandant Daly's splendid exploit in capturing Linen Hall Barracks we all know. You must know also that the whole population, both clergy and laity, of this district are united in his praises. Commandant MacDonagh is established in an impregnable position reaching from the walls of Dublin Castle to Redmond's Hill, and from Bishop Street to Stephen's Green.

(In Stephen's Green, Commandant _____ holds the College of Surgeons, one side of the square, a portion of the other side, and dominates the whole Green and all its entrances and exits).

Commandant de Valera stretches in a position from the Gas Works to Westland Row, holding Boland's Bakery, Boland's Mills, Dublin South-Eastern Railway Works, and dominating Merrion Square.

Commandant Kent holds the South Dublin Union and Guinness's Buildings to Marrowbone Lane, and controls James's Street and district.

On two occasions the enemy effected a lodgement and were driven out with great loss.

The men of North County Dublin are in the field, have occupied all the Police Barracks in the district, destroyed all the telegram system on the Great Northern Railway up to Dundalk, and are operating against the trains of the Midland and Great Western.

Dundalk has sent 200 men to march upon Dublin, and in the other parts of the North our forces are active and growing.

In Galway Captain _____ , fresh after his escape from an Irish prison, is in the field with his men. Wexford and Wicklow are strong, Cork and Kerry are equally acquitting themselves creditably. (We have every confidence that our Allies in Germany and kinsmen in America are straining every nerve to hasten matters on our behalf).

As you know, I was wounded twice yesterday and am unable to move about, but have got my bed moved into the firing line, and, with the assistance of your officers, will be just as useful to you as ever.

Courage, boys, we are winning, and in the hour of our victory let us not forget the splendid women who have everywhere stood by us and cheered us on. Never had man or woman a grander cause, never was a cause more grandly served.

(Signed) James Connolly,
Commandant-General,
Dublin Division.

––––

Manifesto issued by P. H. Pearse on the eve of the surrender. It was written on British government paper bearing the Royal Arms embossed in the top left corner.

> Headquarters, Army of the Irish Republic,
> General Post Office, Dublin,
> 28th April, 1916, 9.30 a.m.

The Forces of the Irish Republic, which was proclaimed in Dublin, on Easter Monday, 24th April, have been in possession of the central part of the capital, since 12 noon on that day. Up to yesterday afternoon Headquarters was in touch with all the main outlying positions, and, despite furious and almost continuous assaults by the British Forces all these positions were then still being held, and the Commandants in charge, were confident of their ability to hold them for a long time.

During the course of yesterday afternoon, and evening, the enemy succeeded in cutting our communications with our other positions in the city, and Headquarters is today isolated.

The enemy has burned down whole blocks of houses, apparently with the object of giving themselves a clear field for the play of artillery and field guns against us. We have been bombarded during the evening and night by shrapnel and machine gun fire, but without material damage to our position, which is of great strength.

We are busy completing arrangements for the final defence of Headquarters, and are determined to hold it while the building lasts.

I desire now, lest I may not have an opportunity later, to pay homage to the gallantry of the soldiers of Irish Freedom who have during the past four days been writing with fire and steel the most glorious chapter in the later history of Ireland. Justice can never be done to their heroism, to their discipline, to their gay and unconquerable spirit in the midst of peril and death.

Let me, who has led them into this, speak in my own, and in my fellow commanders' names, and in the name of Ireland present and to come, their praise, and ask those who come after them to remember them.

For four days they have fought and toiled, almost without cessation, almost without sleep, and in the intervals of fighting they have sung songs of the freedom of Ireland. No man has complained, no man has asked 'why?' Each individual has spent himself, happy to pour out his strength for Ireland and for freedom. If they do not win this fight, they will at least have deserved to win it. But win it they will, although they may win it in death. Already they have won a great thing. They have redeemed Dublin from many shames, and made her name splendid among the names of cities.

If I were to mention the names of individuals, my list would be a long one.

I will mention only that of Commandant-General James Connolly, Commanding the Dublin Division. He lies wounded, but is still the guiding brain of our resistance.

If we accomplish no more than we have accomplished, I am satisfied. I am satisfied that we have saved Ireland's honour. I am satisfied that we should have accomplished more, that we should have accomplished the task of enthroning, as well as proclaiming, the Irish Republic as a Sovereign State, had our arrangements for a simultaneous rising of the whole country, with a combined plan as sound as the Dublin plan has been proved to be, been allowed to go through on Easter Sunday. Of the fatal countermanding order which prevented those plans from being carried out, I will not speak further. Both Eoin MacNeill and we have acted in the best interests of Ireland.

For my part, as to anything I have done in this, I am not afraid to face either the judgment of God, or the judgment of posterity.

(Signed) P. H. Pearse,
Commandant-General.

————

Surrender orders

In order to prevent the further slaughter of Dublin citizens, and in the hope of saving the lives of our followers now surrounded and hopelessly outnumbered, the members of the Provisional Government at present at Headquarters have agreed to an unconditional surrender, and the Commandants of the various districts in the City and Country will order their commands to lay down arms.

P. H. Pearse,

29th April, 1916.

I agree to these conditions for the men only under my own command in the Moore Street District and for the men in the Stephen's Green Command.

James Connolly

April 29/16.

On consultation with Commandant Ceannt and other officers I have decided to agree to unconditional surrender also.

Thomas MacDonagh.

———

Various orders

Dublin Brigade Order.

23rd April, 1916.

H.Q.

1. As publicly announced, the inspection and manoeuvres ordered for this day are cancelled.

2. All Volunteers are to stay in Dublin until further orders.

Thomas MacDonagh,

Commandant.

Ed. de Valera.

Dublin Brigade Order.

H.Q.

24th April, 1916.

1. The four city battalions will parade for inspection and route march at 10 a.m. today. Commandants will arrange centres.

2. Full arms and equipment and one day's rations.

Thomas MacDonagh,

Commandant.

Coy. E will parade at Beresford Place at 10 a.m.

P. H. Pearse,

Commandant.

———

The following is a 'credit' left on the premises of Messrs Alex. Findlater and Company for goods commandeered by the insurgents.

No._____ Date <u>24/4/16.</u> Time_____
                    Place_____
To <u>Alex. Findlater</u>
                    Place_____
Commandeered by the Irish Republic to be paid for goods to the value of about £25.

By Order of the I.R. Government.

———

Commission

'Irish Citizen Army'
Headquarters, Liberty Hall, Dublin.
Commandant James Connolly.
Date, 24th April, 1916.

By warrant of the Army Council, I hereby appoint Michael Kelly to take the rank of Lieutenant, with full powers to exercise all the rights and perform all the duties belonging to that rank.

(Signed) James Connolly,
Commandant.

———

Casualties

The official British list of casualties, which must be read with reserve, is as follows:[103]

	Killed	Wounded	Missing	Total
Military officers	17	46	66	129
Military, other ranks	86	311	9	406
RIC officers	2	—	—	2
RIC, others ranks	12	23	—	35
D.M. Police	3	3	—	6
Civilians and insurgents	180	614	—	794
Totals	300	997	75	1,372

A subsequent list issued under the signature of Sir J. G. Maxwell, the general officer commanding the British forces in Ireland, gives the figures of casualties in the 'other ranks' of the troops as: killed 89, wounded 288.

———

Executions, sentences and internment

Insurgents shot after courts martial	16
Shot without trial	5
Executed in London	1
Total	22

Total numbers of prisoners passed through Richmond Barracks	3,326
Men released	1,104
Sentenced to penal servitude	160
Acquitted by courts martial	26
Men interned	1,862
Women released	72
Women interned	5
Total	3,229
Approximate number of premises in the city destroyed or heavily damaged	214

———

British despatches

Despatch from the Lord Lieutenant, Field Marshal Lord French.

The insurrection broke out in Dublin at 2.15 p.m., on April 24, and by 5.30 p.m., on the same afternoon a considerable force from the Curragh had arrived in Dublin to reinforce the garrison, and other troops were on their way from Athlone, Belfast and Templemore. The celerity with which these reinforcements became available says much for *the arrangements which had been made to meet such a contingency.*

After seeing General Friend, I gave orders for the

movement of two brigades to commence as soon as their transport could be arranged. I am aware that in doing so I was acting beyond the powers which were delegated to me, but I considered the situation to be so critical that it was necessary to act at once without reference to the Army Council.

I beg to bring to your notice the assistance afforded to me by the Lords Commissioners of the Admiralty, who met every request made to them for men, guns and transport, and whose action enabled me to reinforce and maintain the garrison in the South and West of Ireland without unduly drawing upon the troops which it was desirable to retain in England.

Extracts from the despatch of General Maxwell.

In the Commander's absence [Colonel Kennard] the Adjutant had ordered all available troops from Portobello, Richmond and Royal Barracks to proceed to the Castle, and the Sixth Reserve Cavalry Regiment towards Sackville [O'Connell] Street. The fighting strength of British troops available in Dublin at that moment was 2,427 officers and men, made up as follows:

Sixth Cavalry Regiment   35 officers, 851 other ranks.

Third Royal Irish Regiment   18 officers, 385 other ranks.

Tenth Royal Dublin Fusiliers   37 officers, 430 other ranks.

Third Royal Irish Rifles   21 officers, 650 other ranks.

Of these troops, *an inlying picket of 400 men, which for some days past had been held in readiness*, proceeded at once and the remainder followed shortly afterwards.

At 12.30 p.m. a telephone message was sent to General Officer Commanding, Curragh, to *mobilise the mobile column, which had been arranged for to meet any emergency*, and to despatch it dismounted to Dublin by trains which were being sent from Kingsbridge. This column, under the command of Colonel Portal, consisted of 1,600 officers and other ranks from the Third Reserve Cavalry Brigade.

(The italics in both these extracts are mine.)

By Tuesday 25 April, when Brigadier General W. H. M. Lowe assumed the command in Dublin, the total number of British troops under his command was 4,600 officers and men.

Owing to the confusion caused by the countermanding order it is not possible to give even an approximately accurate figure of the number of Volunteers, Citizen Army and Hibernian Rifles who took part in the Dublin Rising. It may be assumed, however, that the initial number did not exceed 2,000 all told.

———

Plan of the Rising

Letter to the Editor, Irish Weekly Independent

Sir,

I have read with great interest the description of the 'Plan' of the Rising of 1916, as set forth in your current issue, by Liam Skinner. For the sake of historical accuracy, I think there is one vital aspect which requires much further elucidation.

He says that the 'Plan' was drafted by Joseph M. Plunkett, 'assisted' by the late Rory O'Connor. The only basis he gives for this is that the late Mr O'Connor was then an engineer in the employment of the Dublin Corporation. If there are any valid grounds for such an assumption I should personally be very glad to be informed of them.

It is a well-known and well established fact that the chief military advisor of the General Staff of the Volunteers was the late Colonel J. J. O'Connell. Yet your contributor makes no mention of this officer in this connection.

It is by no means a difficult matter to re-construct the supposed 'plans' for the Rising from the well-known and fully established march of events. But without some sort of valid evidence, I cannot accept the statement that the late Mr O'Connor had anything whatever to do with the supposed plans.

Apart from the fact that degrees in civil engineering are no warrant whatever for professional skill in strategy and tactics, there were political reasons why it was extremely unlikely that the exclusive inner circle of the I.R.B., would admit an outsider to a knowledge of so vital a matter. That political background is this:

In 1907 the late C. J. Dolan resigned his British Parliamentary seat, and embraced Sinn Fein. This led to a by-election in North Leitrim in February, 1908. At that time there was in existence a body called 'The Young Ireland Branch of the United Irish League'. This was one of the most memorable by-elections ever held. Not only did the Young Irelanders make their political debut in it, but also Sean MacDermott made his first public political appearance as organiser for Sinn Fein.

These Young Irelanders have been described by an I.R.B. contemporary as: 'A combination of youthful place-hunters, who were quite willing to dislodge some of the old big guns, but hoped to persuade the Irish people to change the players'. Amongst those youthful aspirants to British parliamentary honours were: Richard Hazelton, Cruise O'Brien, Sheehy-Skeffington, Tom Kettle, Rory O'Connor and Liam Lynch.

I find it extremely difficult to accept that so cautious and exclusive a body as the inner circle of the I.R.B. would admit anyone with such a political background to an intimate knowledge of their most vital documents. At any rate, if there are valid grounds for the assumption, in the interests of historical truth, your contributor should set them forth.

Dublin.

W. J. Brennan-Whitmore,

Comdt.

There was no reply to this letter.

———

Public notice

Arms and Ammunition

I, General Sir John Grenfell Maxwell, K.C.B., K.C.M.G., C.V.O., D.S.O., Commanding in Chief His Majesty's Forces in Ireland, hereby order that all members of the Irish Volunteer Sinn Fein Organization, or of the Citizen Army, shall forthwith surrender all arms, ammunition and explosives, in their possession to the nearest Military Authority or the nearest Police Barracks.

Any member of either of these organizations found in possession of any arms, ammunition or explosives, after 6th May, 1916, will be severely dealt with.

J. G. Maxwell.

General,

Commanding-in-Chief,

The Forces in Ireland.

Headquarters, Irish Command,

2nd May, 1916.

Notes

Introduction

1. Mairin Ní Dhonnchadha and Theo Dorgan, *Revising the Rising* (Derry, 1991), p. ix.
2. W. J. Brennan-Whitmore, 'My Part in the Easter Rising', *Irish Weekly Independent*, 6 Aug.–3 Sept. 1953. The original version of the current manuscript is in the possession of his daughter Attracta Maher, to whom I am indebted for some of the information in the introduction.
3. There is a comprehensive discussion of the memoirs and secondary works on the Rising between 1916 and 1966 in F. X. Martin's '1916: Myth, Fact and Mystery', *Studia Hibernica*, no. 7, 1967, pp. 1–124. A distinction should be made between accounts by participants and those by other eye-witnesses. For vivid accounts by participants, see Desmond Ryan, *The Rising* (Dublin, 1949); Frank Robbins, *Under the Starry Plough: Recollections of the Irish Citizen Army* (Dublin, 1977); Brian O'Higgins, *The Soldier's Story of Easter Week* (Dublin, 1925); Kathleen Clarke, *Revolutionary Woman: An Autobiography* (Dublin, 1991); Roger McHugh (ed.), *Dublin 1916* (London, 1966); Proinsias Ó Conluain (ed.), *Seán T.: Scéal á Bheatha á insint ag Seán T. Ó Ceallaigh* (Baile Átha Cliath, 1963); Kenneth Griffith and Timothy E. O'Grady, *Curious Journey: An Oral History of Ireland's Unfinished Revolution* (London, 1982); Desmond Fitzgerald, 'Inside the GPO', *Irish Times*, Supplement, 7 April 1966. Personal accounts of several participants were serialised in *An tÓglach* on 16, 23 and 30 January and 6 February 1926. Similar series appeared in the *Capuchin Annual* and *An Cosantóir* in 1966.

    As to accounts by non-participants, the *Irish Times* carried a sporadic citizen's diary at the time of the Rising by J. R. Clegg of Rathgar. It was reprinted in that newspaper, 7 April 1966. The *Sinn Féin Rebellion Handbook* published by the *Weekly Irish Times* in 1917 is still useful. James Stephens's *The Insurrection in Dublin* (New York, 1916; republished, Dublin, 1965 and Gerrard's Cross, 1978), one of the earliest accounts, remains one of the most perceptive. See also, among others, J. J. Leary, daily account in *Saturday Evening Post,* 29 April, 6 and 13 May 1916; Thomas Johnson, diary of the Rising, in Anthony Gaughan, *Thomas Johnson* (Dublin, 1980), pp. 46–57; R. Kain, 'A Diary of Easter Week: One Dubliner's Experience', *Irish University Review,* x, 1980; and most recently, Adrian and Sally Warwick-Haller, *Letters from Dublin, Easter 1916: Alfred Fannin's Diary of the Rising* (Dublin, 1995).

There are numerous unpublished diaries and memoirs. See for example accounts by Dr A. D. Courtney, Breda Grace and Simon Donnelly, De Valera Papers, Killiney, MSS 29E, 34B, 94/385; Douglas Hyde, 'Reflections After Easter Week', TCD MS 10343/7; John Dillon to Lady Mathew, 25 April to 1 May 1916, Dillon Papers, TCD MS 9820. Between 1947 and 1959, the Bureau of Military History took depositions from survivors. These are now preserved in the Department of the Taoiseach. They are still closed to researchers.

4. Eamon de Valera agreed to join the IRB in 1915 but did not attend meetings. Several Volunteer officers were sworn in just before the Rising but Seán T. O'Kelly thought that this may only have happened in Dublin. The Earl of Longford and T. P. O'Neill, *Eamon de Valera* (London, 1974), p. 75; Maureen Wall, 'The Plan and the Countermand: the Country and Dublin', in K. B. Nowlan (ed.), *The Making of 1916* (Dublin, 1969), p. 215; Ó Conluain (ed.), *Seán T.*, p. 156.

5. On the military plans for the Rising see G. A. Hayes-McCoy, 'A Military History of the Rising', in Nowlan (ed.), *Making of 1916*, pp. 255–337; Col. P. J. Hally, 'The Easter Rising in Dublin: the Military Aspects', *Irish Sword*, viii, no. 30 (Summer 1967); John P. Duggan, *A History of the Irish Army* (Dublin, 1991), pp. 1–30.

6. The classic example is Florence O'Donoghue's invaluable edition of Diarmuid Lynch's *The IRB and the 1916 Insurrection* (Cork, 1957) which is largely a commentary on other accounts.

7. For his attitude to constitutionalism see pp. 110 and 148.

8. Brennan-Whitmore's *With the Irish in Frongoch* (Dublin, 1917), which shows signs of having been hurriedly written 'in the leisure hours of

three weeks of the life of a working journalist', has proved an invaluable source. See also Sean O'Mahony, *Frongoch: University of Revolution* (Dublin, 1987) which makes considerable use of Brennan-Whitmore's account.

9. *Defence Forces, Saorstát Éireann, 1926: Army List and Directory*, edited by Commandant W. J. Brennan-Whitmore (An tÓglach Office, Dublin, 1926).

Ante-scriptum

10. On the development of the Irish Volunteers, see F. X. Martin, *The Irish Volunteers, 1913–15* (Dublin, 1963).

11. Brennan-Whitmore and Ginger O'Connell became lifelong friends. See for example Brennan-Whitmore's glowing tributes on O'Connell's intelligence reports in 1924. Reports and Correspondence re Military Customs Brigade, National Library of Ireland, MS 22133.

12. For a more detailed account of Connolly's relationship with militant nationalism and his enrolment in the IRB in January 1916, see Austen Morgan, *James Connolly: A Political Biography* (Manchester, 1988), pp. 139–95.

13. O'Casey objected to Markievicz's membership of the Volunteers which he saw as a rival middle-class organisation, many of the members of which had failed to support labour in 1913. In autumn 1914, when his proposal that she be forced to choose between the Irish Citizen Army (ICA) and the Volunteers was rejected, he resigned as secretary of the Citizen Army. As he was no longer involved, it is somewhat harsh to suggest that he 'certainly shirked' the Rising. Ibid., p. 145; Robbins, *Under the Starry Plough*, pp. 19–20. For O'Casey's own account, see P. O'Cathasaigh (Sean O'Casey), *The Story of the Irish Citizen Army* (Dublin, 1919), pp. 44–6 and 'Sean O'Casey's Easter' (reprinted from his autobiography) in McHugh (ed.), *Dublin 1916*, pp. 240–58. On his attitude to Markievicz, see Martin, '1916: Myth, Fact and Mystery', pp. 81–2.

14. For the Irish Transvaal Committee, see Richard Davis, *Arthur Griffith and Non-Violent Sinn Féin* (Dublin, 1974), pp. 38–9.

15. For Connolly's thinking on insurrection and street-fighting, see *Worker's Republic*, 29 May, 5, 12, 19 June, 3, 10, 17 July 1915.

16. Although the textbook was never published, it formed the basis for Brennan-Whitmore's Frongoch lectures in military tactics.

Chapter 1

17. Brennan-Whitmore was wise to exercise such caution as he was under police observation. See, for example, County Inspector's Report, January, PRO, CO 904/99 which notices his activities.
18. In his 1953 account, Brennan-Whitmore correctly stated that Oakley Road was in Ranelagh. *Irish Weekly Independent*, 6 Aug. 1953. It was in the Rathmines-Rathgar urban district. *Thom's Dublin Directory, 1916*, p. 1875.
19. MacDonagh was lecturer in English literature at UCD. Donagh MacDonagh, 'Plunkett and MacDonagh', in F. X. Martin (ed.), *Leaders and Men of the Easter Rising, Dublin, 1916* (London, 1967), p. 173.
20. Nathan was Jewish but hardly German. His great-great-grandfather had migrated from Germany to England in the late eighteenth century. There is no evidence that Nathan ever seriously contemplated what Brennan-Whitmore suggests. For Nathan, see Anthony Haydon, *Sir Matthew Nathan: British Colonial Governor and Civil Servant* (Brisbane, 1976) and Leon Ó Broin, *Dublin Castle and the 1916 Rising* (London, 1966) which is based largely on the Nathan Papers in the Bodleian Library, Oxford.
21. On MacNeill, see F. X. Martin and F. J. Byrne (eds.), *The Scholar Revolutionary* (Shannon, 1973).
22. Brennan-Whitmore is certainly correct about the firmness of the resolve of the majority of the IRB leadership. It is less certain how many of them shared the blood sacrifice viewpoint. See J. J. Lee, *Ireland 1912–1985* (Cambridge, 1989), p. 25; Lynch, *The IRB*, pp. 52–4; Clarke, *Revolutionary Woman*, pp. 74–7.
23. On Casement and the *Aud*, see R. McHugh, 'Casement and German help', in Martin (ed.), *Leaders and Men*, pp. 177–89.
24. It is incorrect to say the authorities were taken completely by surprise; they had anticipated the Rising but were then misled into delaying action by the countermanding order. See Ó Broin, *Dublin Castle*, pp. 81–8; Leon Ó Broin, *The Chief Secretary: Augustine Birrell*

in Ireland (London, 1969), pp. 171–5. For Birrell's own account, see *Things Past Redress* (London, 1937), pp. 193–236.

25. Although Brennan-Whitmore continued to believe that this document was authentic, it is now widely accepted that it was a forgery, probably by Plunkett or MacDermott. See Lynch, *The IRB*, pp. 134–5; Nowlan (ed.), *Making of 1916*, p. 16. The Royal Commission on the Rebellion suggested that it was printed in Liberty Hall. *Royal Commission on the Rebellion in Ireland, Report* [Cd 8279], House of Commons, 1916, p. 12.

Chapter 2

26. See above, note 22. Brennan-Whitmore may underestimate the differences in personality and temperament between Pearse, MacDonagh and Plunkett on one hand and Clarke and MacDermott on the other.

27. The surmise that the fund was no more than a wild rumour is undoubtedly correct. No credible evidence to the contrary has ever emerged.

28. Plunkett visited Algeria where he studied Arabic literature and language for a short time. MacDonagh, 'Plunkett and MacDonagh', in Martin (ed.), *Leaders and Men*, pp. 168–9.

29. On the military plan for the Rising, see above, note 5. For Connolly's view of street-fighting, see note 15.

30. For a short account of events in Wexford during the Rising, see testimony of County Inspector John Robert Sharpe, RIC, Wexford, to the Royal Commission. *Royal Commission on the Rebellion in Ireland, Evidence* [Cd 8311], House of Commons, 1916, pp. 82–3.

31. The date of this meeting is unclear but assuming it was shortly before the Rising, Brennan-Whitmore's account clarifies an uncertainty on the part of Mellowes's biographer regarding his movements at this time. C. Desmond Greaves, *Liam Mellowes and the Irish Revolution* (London, 1971), p. 82. Mellowes spent much of his boyhood in Wexford with his maternal grandparents. His aunt Julia Jordan married Robert Whitmore.

32. This view is shared by many commentators. See Hally, 'The Easter Rising', pp. 320–1. As Brennan-Whitmore suggests (page 57), St

Stephen's Green was dangerously exposed. However, for a counterargument, see Robbins, *Under The Starry Plough*, pp. 92–101. There is a graphic account of events in the St Stephen's Green area in the 1916 memoirs of Breda Grace and Dr A. D. Courtney, De Valera Papers, Killiney, MSS 94/385, and in the Easter week diary of Douglas Hyde who lived on Earlsfort Terrace. TCD, MS 10343/7.

33. On Connolly's 'arrest' see Lynch, *The IRB*, p. 94; C. Desmond Greaves, *The Life and Times of James Connolly* (London, 1961), p. 316; and note 12 above.

34. When Connolly returned after his 'arrest', he would only say that he had been 'walking in the country'. Morgan, *Connolly*, p. 169.

35. Griffith was invited to join the supreme council of the IRB in 1914 but declined. He was named as a member of the proposed civil provisional government by the IRB in 1916. He did not know of the plans for the Rising until Saturday 22 April. He disapproved and hoped that MacNeill's countermanding order would prevent a Rising. However there is some evidence to support Brennan-Whitmore's suggestion that he then sought to join the rebels but was told that his work lay elsewhere. Sean Ó Lúing, 'Arthur Griffith and Sinn Féin', in Martin (ed.), *Leaders and Men*, pp. 2–3. On Griffith's activities during Easter week, see also Ó Lúing, *Art Ó Gríofa* (Dublin, 1953), pp. 247–67.

Chapter 3

36. Since Brennan-Whitmore wrote this the release of Dublin Castle records has confirmed this view. See Ó Broin, *Dublin Castle*, p. 82.

37. Brennan-Whitmore's references to the military council of the Volunteers are confusing because of the existence of a military council of the IRB. The Volunteers had a council and an executive. In addition there were meetings of the headquarters staff. The countermanding order on the Saturday was signed by MacNeill as chief of staff.

38. This banner first appeared in 1914 and was removed by the authorities in December 1914. Morgan, *Connolly*, p. 150.

39. As well as being indecisive, Birrell was frequently absent from Ireland. Ó Broin, *The Chief Secretary*, pp. 136–70.

40. De Valera had been appointed commandant in March 1915.

41. Although de Valera's insistence on signed orders was characteristic, it was not wholly unreasonable given the very confused situation. When the countermanding orders of the chief of staff had been delivered to him in a personal letter, de Valera told MacNeill he would only obey orders countersigned by his immediate superior, MacDonagh. When Pearse's order to surrender was conveyed to him he hesitated as it was not countersigned by MacDonagh and he feared a trick. Longford and O'Neill, *De Valera*, pp. 36 and 45.

42. Brian O'Higgins's own account of the Rising, *The Soldier's Story*, does not refer to this issue but he describes the struggle as one for faith and fatherland and records the fact that he and some of his colleagues on the roof of the GPO recited the rosary 'almost every half-hour of the four days and four nights we were on the roof' (pp. 43–50). In the 1930s and 1940s, he expounded on this theme repeatedly in the pages of the *Wolfe Tone Annual* which he edited. The faith and fatherland theme was first popularised by J. J. O'Kelly (Sceilg) in the pages of the *Catholic Bulletin* which he edited. Brennan-Whitmore was a regular contributor to the *Catholic Bulletin* before the Rising (see vol. iv, Jan. and June 1914, pp. 36–40, 393–9).

43. On Plunkett and the pope, see, Martin, '1916: Myth, Fact and Mystery', pp. 112–17. See also John H. Whyte, '1916: Revolution and Religion', in Martin (ed.), *Leaders and Men*, pp. 215–26.

44. Plunkett had had an operation on his throat in Switzerland. Leon Ó Broin states that Collins spent the previous night with Plunkett at the Metropole. Ó Broin, *Michael Collins* (Dublin, 1980), p. 16. T. P. Coogan, relying on Margery Forester, *The Lost Leader* (London, 1971), pp. 402, states that Collins transferred Plunkett from the nursing home on the Friday night but then recounts Brennan-Whitmore's version of the incident at the hotel on the Monday morning. Coogan, *Michael Collins* (London, 1990), p. 37.

45. See above, note 4.

46. For slightly different versions of the genesis of the Proclamation, see Clarke, *Revolutionary Woman*, pp. 69–70; Lynch, *The IRB*, p. 104.

47. O'Rahilly's car was already laden with rifles which he had brought with him. Aodagán O'Rahilly, *Winding the Clock: O'Rahilly and the 1916 Rising* (Dublin, 1991), p. 206.

48. Ruth Dudley Edwards tentatively identifies this woman as Pearse's sister Mary Brigid. Edwards, *Patrick Pearse: The Triumph of Failure* (London, 1977), pp. 277 and 359. Another source records O'Rahilly's sister, Anna, as having approached Pearse at this time and berated him about the course of events. Whether the two stories are related is unclear. O'Rahilly, *Winding the Clock*, pp. 205–7.

Chapter 4

49. For other accounts of the march from Liberty Hall to the GPO, see Ryan, *The Rising*, p. 124 and Lynch's commentary, *The IRB*, p. 140. Lynch questions Ryan and Brennan-Whitmore's assertion that an order 'Left turn' was given.

50. The details of the arrest of Lieutenant Chalmers were the subject of yet another dispute between Desmond Ryan (*The Rising*, p. 124) who mentions Brennan-Whitmore's involvement and D. Lynch (*The IRB*, p. 141) who does not. See also *Sinn Féin Rebellion Handbook*, p. 13.

51. MacDermott did not have a command. He and Clarke made their own way from Liberty Hall to the GPO and spent the duration of the week there. Lynch, *The IRB*, p. 144. MacDermott was not a soldier but as the week progressed he played a more active role. See Charles J. Travers, 'Sean MacDiarmada, 1883–1916', *Breifne*, 1966, pp. 1–46.

52. Desmond Ryan, Pearse's former pupil, was foremost amongst those who assigned Pearse the place of honour. His works include *The Man Called Pearse* (Dublin, 1918); *Remembering Sion* (Dublin, 1938); and, most influential of all, *The Rising*.

53. The Royal Commission on the Rebellion was told that the Metropole was raided for food ten minutes after the occupation of the GPO. *Evidence*, p. 8.

54. There were it seems two groups of lancers. One was returning to Marlborough Barracks from escort duty; this group was fired on at Ormond Quay. The second group, fired on from the GPO, had been called out of Marlborough Barracks. This group came from the north end of O'Connell Street. Hayes-McCoy, 'A Military History of the Rising', p. 268; Lynch, *The IRB*, p. 106; *Sinn Féin Rebellion Handbook*, p. 12.

55. Ryan, *The Rising*, p. 132, mentions the attempt to blow up Nelson Pillar. Lynch, *The IRB*, p. 145, gives a third explanation—the intention was to blow down the tram lines.

56. See above, note 32.

57. The precise intentions regarding Dublin Castle are still unclear. Robbins, *Under the Starry Plough*, pp. 98–9; Hayes-McCoy, 'A Military History of the Rising', pp. 263–4.

58. Rex Taylor, *Michael Collins* (London, 1958).

59. Although Brennan-Whitmore admired Pearse the visionary, there are echoes here and on pp. 82–3 of Collins's contrast of Pearse and Connolly (ibid., p. 77) and Tom Clarke's exasperated cry in the GPO that someone should get Pearse a desk with paper and pens and set him down to write (Clarke, *Revolutionary Woman*, p. 79).

60. As Brennan-Whitmore's argument here seems to rest on his not having seen O'Kelly, it cannot be conclusive. Seán T. O'Kelly's own account was serialised in the *Irish Press*, 6–9 Aug. 1961, while Brennan-Whitmore was completing his memoir. It was later published in book form in Irish in 1963. He recounts his part in the occupation of the GPO and his various errands, including the releasing of Hobson. Ó Conluain (ed.), *Seán T.*, pp. 166–91. O'Kelly's account has been used by many historians. For example, Ruth Dudley Edwards states that Connolly sent a group led by O'Kelly to break up the mobs who were looting (*Pearse*, p. 286). His accuracy on various details has been questioned by F. X. Martin but not specifically his account of his participation in the occupation ('1916: Myth, Fact and Mystery', pp. 98–9). O'Kelly's future wife Phyllis Ryan and her sister and brother all served in the GPO.

61. Lynch's 'Report on Operations, GPO Garrison Area, Easter Week, 1916' also gives the time for this as 10.00 p.m. Lynch, *The IRB*, p. 163.

Chapter 5

62. Noblett's corner was a well-known landmark. Noblett's Ltd, wholesale confectioners, was located at 34 Sackville Street (they also had a shop in Grafton Street) on the junction with North Earl Street. It stood at the end of Lower Sackville Street—the address of the building on the opposite side of the North Earl Street intersection

(Tyler's Boot Manufacturers) was no. 1 Upper Sackville Street. The Pillar Cafe was upstairs in 33 Lower Sackville Street. *Thom's Dublin Directory, 1916*, pp. 1680–2.

63. Noblett's and Lewers & Co. were later reported looted. It was also reported that a pub on North Earl Street was looted 'and when the looters had partaken of the ardent spirits some of them beat each other with the bottles so violently that they were under the necessity of having their wounds dressed in hospital'. *Sinn Féin Rebellion Handbook*, p. 12. Brian O'Higgins recounts how when a priest demanded from a barefoot boy where he got the high-class boots he was carrying, the youth replied: 'In Earl St., Father, but you'll have to hurry up, or they'll all be gone.' *The Soldier's Story*, pp. 39–41. On the looting, see also Max Caulfield, *Easter Rebellion* (Dublin, 1995), pp. 149–50. Caulfield relies a good deal on Brennan-Whitmore's earlier memoirs.

64. As this building assumes an importance later, it is worth seeking to identify it. There was no public house of that name on North Earl Street (although it is not unusual for a pub to be known by a name other than the licence holder's). No. 4 North Earl Street (four doors down from Noblett's) was owned by Philip Meagher who is listed as a vintner in *Thom's* (p. 1555) and in the *Sinn Féin Rebellion Handbook*, p. 37. The report of Captain Purcell, chief of Dublin Fire Brigade, mentions that there were two public houses on North Earl Street, Nagle's and Sheridan's. Ibid., p. 33. Nagle's (now Madigan's) was no. 25 and Sheridan's (owned by Mrs Elizabeth Sheridan) which was also a grocer's was next door at no. 26. However both of these are further along towards Marlborough Street and on the opposite side of the road from Noblett's. As the public house becomes the escape route from the Imperial Hotel and Noblett's out on to North Earl Street, that leaves Meagher's as the only possibility. That site is now occupied by Guiney's.

65. On Cumann na mBan and some of the women of 1916, see Brian Farrell, 'Markievicz and the Women of the Revolution', in the inappropriately named *Leaders and Men of the Easter Rising, Dublin, 1916*, pp. 227–39; Countess Markievicz, 'Women in the Fight', reprinted in McHugh (ed.), *Dublin 1916*, pp. 122–6; Margaret Ward, *In*

their Own Voice: Women and Irish Nationalism (Dublin, 1995), pp. 35–70.

66. There were at least four drapers on the street: O'Reilly's (11–12), Boyce & Co. (20–22), Hickey & Co. (23–4) and M. Rowe & Co. (28; proprietor James Kelly). As O'Reilly's and Boyce's were not in residence and Hickey's was a very large concern which included a furniture warehouse at Cathedral Street, James Kelly may have been the draper referred to. *Thom's*, pp. 1555–6.

67. British troops moving westward from the dock area did occupy Amiens Street station on Monday night. Hayes-McCoy, 'A Military History of the Rising', p. 272. Ryan states that a sniper from Amiens Street fired on rebel positions in O'Connell Street during Monday night. Ryan, *The Rising*, p. 135.

68. The Imperial Hotel (owned by Clery's) and Clery Ltd occupied 21–27 Lower Sackville Street. The premises between there and Noblett's at no. 34 were as follows: 28. Richard Allen (gentleman's tailor and supplier of motor garments and servant's livery); 29. Frs O'Farrell (tobacco and cigar importers), Norman Dewar (photographer), National Standard Life Assurance Company and Peter Donnelly (coal merchant); 30. Munster & Leinster Bank; 31. Cable Boot Co. Ltd, Cole's Dental Surgery, Irish Pig Dealers' Association (secretary, John K. O'Kelly); 32. Dunne & Co. (hat makers), W. F. Brown (window ticket and show card writer), All-Ireland Servants Registry Office and Governesses Agency (proprietor, Kathleen Garrity), Mary Brady (ladies' costumes); 33. Lewers & Co. (boys' clothiers and outfitters), Pillar Cafe Restaurant and Tea Rooms (manager, Miss McFarland). *Thom's*, pp. 1680–2.

Chapter 6

69. The Camp Register shows that he was reunited with many members of the Ferns Company at Frongoch. For a list of the Ferns/Clonee/ Camolin prisoners, see O'Mahony, *Frongoch*, pp. 212–13.

70. For movements of the British military at this time, see Hayes-McCoy, 'A Military History of the Rising', pp. 274–80.

71. The British tactic of dividing the rebel forces north and south of the river made such a lateral attack more likely. Ibid., p. 278.

72. This incident is recalled by Ryan (*The Rising*, p. 131) but he was presumably using Brennan-Whitmore's account.

73. On ICA training see R. M. Fox, *History of the Irish Citizen Army* (London, 1944), pp. 101–19. The leading role assigned to Connolly and the ICA by R. M. Fox rankled with members of the IRB like Diarmuid Lynch and many Volunteers including, evidently, Brennan-Whitmore. See Martin, '1916: Myth, Fact and Mystery', pp. 78–9.

74. A description of the break-in at Lawrence's shop on Easter Tuesday can be found in 'The Personal Experience of Miss Lily Stokes During the Sinn Féin Rebellion of 1916', De Valera Papers, MS 94/385, also printed in McHugh (ed.), *Dublin 1916*, pp. 63–80.

75. Brennan-Whitmore omits here an incident he describes in his earlier account of a boy dressed for golf, teeing up and driving off in O'Connell St. This may be because he did not witness the event himself. An almost identical incident is recorded in A. D. Courtney's reminiscences but the event is located on Baggot St. 'Reminiscences of Easter Rising by Dr A. D. Courtney', De Valera Papers, MS 94/385.

76. Other accounts suggest that Connolly sent out a group to break up the looting. See above, note 60.

Chapter 7

77. The 'Report on Operations, Easter Week 1916' confirms the reinforcement of Brennan-Whitmore's garrison. Lynch, *The IRB*, p. 169.

78. Trinity College had been secured against the rebels on Monday by members of the Dublin University Officers Training Corps. By 7.00 p.m., the garrison there stood at 44. Trinity was of considerable importance in the strategy of dividing the rebels north and south of the river. Brennan-Whitmore is correct in saying that large numbers of troops were brought into TCD on the Wednesday and the college became headquarters for operations. Hayes-McCoy, 'A Military History of the Rising', pp. 272 and 278.

79. These quotations are from the *Sinn Féin Rebellion Handbook* compiled by the *Weekly Irish Times* and published in 1917 (pp. 8–10).

80. See above, note 54.

81. On the Trinity snipers, see *Sinn Féin Rebellion Handbook*, p. 20; 'Inside Trinity College', *Blackwood's Magazine*, July 1916, reprinted in McHugh (ed.), *Dublin 1916*, pp. 158–75.

Chapter 8

82. For the devastation caused by fires during Easter week including the North Earl Street area and the difficulty faced by the fire fighters, see the report by Captain Purcell, chief of Dublin Fire Brigade. *Sinn Féin Rebellion Handbook*, pp. 33–8.

83. There was open ground in Fairview but it is doubtful whether it represented an ideal escape route. Reinforcements had been brought in from the north by rail and, by midweek, there was a strong British military presence in the area. The rebels had controlled Ballybough and Annesley bridges and some surrounding houses at the start of the Rising but they had been dislodged.

84. Regarding 'Fagan's', see above, note 64. The Imperial Hotel backed on to Earl Place which led on to North Earl Street.

85. For a GPO view of the evacuation, see 'Report on Operations, Easter Week 1916', Lynch, *The IRB*, p. 175.

Chapter 9

86. Born in Louth, Frank Thornton (1891–1965) trained the Irish Volunteers in Liverpool. Although Ryan says that he participated in the occupation of the GPO, Lynch states that he remained in Liberty Hall and joined the GPO garrison on Monday afternoon. Lynch, *The IRB*, pp. 140, 145. Thornton later became director of the New Ireland Assurance Company, among other companies. For extracts from Thornton's memoir of 1916 which is in the Bureau of Military History, see Coogan, *Collins*, p. 46.

87. Brennan-Whitmore seems to assume that there was only one sniper firing on their position from Trinity. There were at least two. *Sinn Féin Rebellion Handbook*, p. 20.

88. In his report on the 'great fire' which engulfed the whole area, the chief of Dublin Fire Brigade was unclear where it started but describes in detail how it spread towards and through North Earl Street. *Sinn Féin Rebellion Handbook*, pp. 38–9. It is clear from this

report that Brennan-Whitmore is not overstating the impact of the fire on his command post. Fr John Flanagan who witnessed the conflagration from across the road in the GPO recalled that it was 'a sublime and appalling spectacle'. 'Two Priests: George O'Neill sJ & John Flanagan cc', McHugh (ed.), *Dublin 1916*, p. 191.

Chapter 10

89. Fr John Flanagan of the pro-Cathedral acted as unofficial chaplain to the GPO at Pearse's request. He was in the GPO at this time. Fr William Doherty, another pro-Cathedral priest, had already been rebuffed because of his reputed pro-British sympathies. The priest mentioned by Brennan-Whitmore may have been Fr Doherty or one of the other priests at St Mary's presbytery. These were Frs R. F. Bowden, Adm., Myles Ronan, Laurence Sheehan and Joseph McArdle. Ibid., pp. 183–94; *Thom's*, p. 1031.

90. There were, of course, other routes to Fairview, but all carried the same hazards. At this point they were probably on Waterford Street (which becomes Railway Street) or Gloucester (now Sean MacDermott) Street, which runs parallel. Either street would have brought them to the North Strand but would have involved crossing the railway, which was by now almost certainly well protected and dangerously close to Amiens Street, which was heavily garrisoned.

91. The Lemass brothers, Noel (19) and Seán (17), had gone walking in the Dublin mountains on Easter Monday. Returning via Rathfarnham, they heard of the rebellion from Eoin MacNeill. They walked from there to Jacob's factory but failed to make contact with the garrison inside. The following morning, without a word to their parents, they left their home in Capel Street and reported to the Four Courts. When they were told their battalion (the third) was in the Ringsend area, they set off for there via O'Connell Street. At the GPO they met a friend, Hugh Holohan, on sentry duty so they joined that garrison instead. Noel was sent across the road to join the men in the Imperial Hotel. His brother later seems to have believed he was wounded there rather than after the evacuation. Noel Lemass was killed in the Civil War. Seán Lemass, 'I Remember 1916', *Studies*, LV, 1966, pp. 7–9.

92. In fact the basement they were in can have been on neither as he describes sending two men round the corner to gain entry to the nearest house, perhaps in Gloucester Place. Presumably the discussion centred on the street they had just left which, whether it was Gloucester or Railway, would have brought them to the North Strand.

93. Some of his garrison had indeed made it back to the GPO. Lynch, *The IRB*, p. 175.

Chapter 11

94. The closest name to this in the 1916 Roll of Honour in the National Museum is Matthew Flanagan. The list of prisoners removed from Richmond Barracks to Stafford on 30 April includes one M. Flanigan, 14 St Clement's Road, Drumcondra and three Flanagans from Moore Street. *Sinn Féin Rebellion Handbook*, p. 71.

95. Calvinism made much less impact in England than Scotland.

Chapter 12

96. There were colonial soldiers operating as snipers from Trinity. However the only Australian I have found listed was one 9435, Pte McHugh, 9th Australian Infantry Force. *Sinn Féin Rebellion Handbook*, pp. 20 and 252. It seems unlikely that Brennan-Whitmore would mistake a private for a sergeant.

Chapter 13

97. Irish regiments were used in the fighting, particularly early in the week. The bulk of the fighting later in the week was done by reinforcements from British regiments. Hayes-McCoy, 'A Military History of the Rising', pp. 255–304.

98. The list of prisoners removed from Richmond to Knutsford includes one 'William Whitmore, Clonee, Camolin, Co. Wexford—Farmer'. *Sinn Féin Rebellion Handbook*, p. 75.

99. Crofts and Thornton had been marched to Kilmainham in company with Harry Boland and Sean MacDermott. Coogan, *Collins*, p. 46. They were tried on Thursday 11 May. Thornton was still using the name Frank Drennan. Ibid., p. 66.

100. The list of prisoners issued on 12 May gives the date of their removal from Richmond Barracks as a day earlier than Brennan-Whitmore states (2 May not 3 May), arriving at Knutsford on 3 May. *Sinn Féin Rebellion Handbook*, p. 73.

Appendix

101. With the exception of the letter to the *Irish Weekly Independent*, all of the documents included by Brennan-Whitmore were taken from the *Sinn Féin Rebellion Handbook*. See pp. 1, 44, 48–52.
102. The Dublin Bread Company and Reis & Co. were located at 6–7 and 10 Lower Sackville Street respectively, on the same side as Noblett's.
103. The official list of casualties used by Brennan-Whitmore is taken from the list issued on 11 May 1916 with the only difference being his inclusion of 66 under the heading 'Military officers missing'. The list of dead is misleading as many wounded died after 11 May.

Index